W9-BSV-206

ROMANCE AFTER SIXTY

What Men Think They Want

MINERVA H. NEIDITZ, Ph.D.

To Lee,
Minerva Neiditz

ACKNOWLEDGEMENTS:

I thank the 140 men I interviewed who spent hours on the phone with me, revealing their wishes and experiences. I especially thank Murray Korngold whose comments were inspirational and whose encouragement was particularly valuable. I, of course, thank my partner and friend, Jack Calkins, for writing the first chapter and for the years of wonderful, romantic friendship that came out of this process. I've also foisted the book on many readers who have given me suggestions for revision: Kathleen Spivack, Gene Gaddis, Matt Proser, Florence Snyder, Penelope Queen, my brother, Milton Heller, Francesca Johnson, Edward Simpson, Jerome Lord, Anne Edelstein, who tried to find a publisher, Millie Geetter, Maria Matthiessen, Iris Cornell, Barbara Wasserman, Dr. Bernard Starr, Walter Rabetz, whose photograph of me appears in the back of this book, his wife, Marilyn Rabetz, who helped me more than anyone should to put together this pre-publication edition for my 50th Smith College Reunion, and many, many others.

I have protected the confidentiality of my interviewees by changing their names and locations and professions whenever necessary. I did not intend to harm anyone with my reactions, but I wanted to reveal what I have observed in as truthful a manner as possible. I meant this book to be much like Chaucer's Canterbury Tales. I don't believe that anyone would want to sue Chaucer for satirizing his taletellers.

TABLE OF CONTENTS:

The interviews:

INTRODUCTION:

Who should read this book?

Are you curious about the lives and loves of older single men? What do you think they want in their next relationship? Do they want what younger men want? Do many want to remarry? Or do the women they have met disappoint them? Are they overwhelmed by aggressive women pursuing what's left of a small minority? Do they avoid dependent women who want to be taken care of? Do they prefer independent, self-reliant types? Do they want a nurse with a purse? Companionship? Younger women? Are they hoping to fall in love? Or do they want, above all, to remain single?

Are you a single woman who thinks there's no one out there worth dating? Do you subscribe to the adage: "The odds aren't good and the goods are odd?" Have you found too many Mr. Wrongs? Do you want someone to talk to or do things with? Have you been looking for a sugar daddy to pay the bills? Do you desire great sex or a "grand" passion? Are you hoping to fall in love? Have you nursed a sick husband for ages and decided once is enough? Or have you always been single and wondered what you're missing? Do you, above all, want to remain single?

Are you married and worried about what might happen if your spouse were to die? Are you concerned about an older parent who is widowed or divorced and is without a companion? Do you know older people who are struggling with loneliness? Do you know older people whose relationships have failed because of the baggage they have carried into new love affairs? Or are you just a lover of stories about the human condition in the last quarter of life's spectrum?

If you've answered yes to any of these questions, this book is for you because it will entertain and instruct you. I cannot guarantee that you will find someone. This book is not riddled with statistics that are unproven and unprovable. But you will learn about a variety of single men who are "out there" following new rules, creating new paradigms, looking for adventures and a happiness they had not planned for. Because of greater life expectancy and changes in attitudes about sex, you will learn to update your views about why and where and how to find a good man.

Consciously you will define your preferences, re-examine your myths about marriage, love, and spiritual renewal. You will also be given the opportunity to recognize men who are dangerous or poor choices for a stable relationship.

You will chuckle at some of my mishaps as a veteran of the "seeking" phase. Of course, it's not easy to find someone to love who also loves you. Otherwise, there would be fewer songs about that process. Knowing another human being is an adventure. This broadening of experience, meeting all types of people, can be a joyous undertaking. If you seek with tongue in cheek, there's the possibility for laughter and expansion of your spirit.

I have interviewed in depth over 120 men in the last two years: rich men, poor men, beggar men and/or thieves, doctors, lawyers and corporate chiefs. I have also dated at least 20 men in the last 22 years. That makes 140 men. Four of these 20 men have been serious relationships. I've learned a lot about my preferences and theirs. We've had some wonderful moments and we've also experienced sorrow. I don't regret meeting most of them, regardless of the endings.

What Do These Men Say They Want?

I am going to tell you their true stories. You can decide for yourself if any of these men could be people you'd like to meet. In some cases, you'll decide, I hope, to avoid a small number of them. My first and most important question to the men I interviewed was: What do you want most in your next relationship? Describe the woman you're looking for.

When I tell my friends what I'm doing, they all ask, "So what do they want?" I have to answer, "They want different types of women depending upon whom they've known." This book is not about simplistic stereotyping, attempting to help you in your efforts to understand the "other."

However, I do offer some generalizations based on my skewed sample and I do group the men in meaningful clusters. I use Chaucer's model of a pilgrimage, but only two of the men are seeking God in the form of cosmic consciousness and an abstract ideal. The others are seeking an equally elusive, modern goal, a permanent relationship that is mutually satisfying.

Like Chaucer, I am more interested in each man's individuality than in any arbitrary label. Also like Chaucer, I tend to dispel myths. For example, most of the men were not looking for younger women, despite that common perception. One doctor told me he had a *war* test. If he mentioned *the* war and the woman thought it was Vietnam, she was too young for him. I am aware that many men do want younger women when they first get divorced. I know a 65 year old who slept with girls in their twenties and thirties for three or four months. But he remarried an older woman close to his age because she knew his songs, his history and his background. He didn't share the interests of the "young ones" except the desire to prove he could still "get it up."

Nor did I talk to men who said they were looking for a nurse with a purse. Usually they gave a list of qualities that described femininity: soft, gentle, affectionate, demonstrative, sensual, fun to be with, etc. Many did talk about companionship, but they were seeking "travel companions" who would be adventuresome, not stay-at-home types.

No one talked about finding an equal, although many were seeking intelligent women. Only one man said he was looking for a woman with imagination. He was an artist.

Most of them mentioned they wanted women who could see the world as they do. They are not looking for women who are exotic, foreign, captivating in their strangeness. Some said that they want women who share their perspective, their worldview. Others talked to me about having had wives who argued with them. They've decided they don't want such trouble anymore.

I mentioned this conclusion to some friends and the husband said, "That's not why I married my second wife. She never agrees with me." "I don't agree with you," she promptly injected, beginning her version of why they had married. There may be a discrepancy between what men want and what they get. I am simply recounting what single, older men said about their conscious motives.

You are probably thinking, "I know what they want. They want sex." Of course, many do emphasize sex, but more of them insist upon brains. The man who was looking for a woman with imagination became my close friend. Because he was an artist, he was supportive of my work. We dated for almost a year. What finally ended our relationship was his stinginess. When I asked him why he never brought me flowers, he retorted, " Do you know how much a rose costs? $3.95!" I have gone out with men who order only one dinner and offer me half. One man I dated asked what I wanted for my birthday. I said I wanted a tennis racket. He replied he would buy me "half a racket." These men are not necessarily poor. They suffer from a poverty mentality.

This trait of stinginess often was linked to a lack of generosity toward others, a withholding pattern that may have started in childhood. Few of these men were idealistic or philanthropic. Only one man had started an organization to help teen-age boys who were in trouble. One architect had been involved in the civil rights movement and was ending his life trying to establish a spiritual retreat. I felt some idealism in a few of the doctors I interviewed, but one doctor who was Lutheran asked me if I was a Lutheran. When I said no, he refused to talk to me.

"I only talk to Lutherans," he explained.

You'll be surprised to learn that he was the only man who refused to talk to me. All the others were eager to tell their stories. They welcomed the opportunity to talk about themselves to a sympathetic audience. I assured them that I would change their names and disguise them to protect their identities. I did not give out my telephone number. Nor did I encourage any of them to call me back.

But one man was struck by the possibility that I might read his book reports. After all, I had a Ph.D. in English. He found me through a directory on the Internet. He had insisted on knowing my last name. For months he sent me neatly typed assessments of the latest books he was reading. I became a desirable, receptive mind in his active fantasy life.

Yes, many of these men were lonely. They were delighted to reveal all, while I paid for the phone bill.

Often I heard idiosyncratic answers: "I want a woman who will follow me to the grave." "I want a woman who has never heard of Jesus and doesn't talk to him three times a day." "I want a woman who can fit into my jigsaw puzzle just as my first wife did." "I want a woman who's silent, a deaf-mute." "I want a woman who's modest, who won't undress in front of me." "I want a woman with a heritage like mine, a family that came over on the Mayflower or its equivalent." "I want a woman who can fit into my antique bathtub for two." "I want a woman who will not chop down my favorite tree." "I want a woman who will not insult my family."

These quirky responses were all based on what had happened to them in the past or on values that revealed their personalities. Despite these idiosyncratic requirements, I found many men, both divorced and widowers, who wanted to remarry or to have permanent, unmarried relationships: good men, substantial, intelligent, interesting men. They do exist and they are looking for good women, substantial, intelligent, interesting women.

Where Did I Find These Men?

I found the 120 men I talked to on the phone through three dating services: "Single Wordsmiths," "Single Adventurous Voyagers" and "The Best and the

Brightest." These are fictional names for real services. In fact, you must send a diploma or graduate certificate to the latter service to prove you're an alum of a brand name college. I paid $2 or $3 for each profile. I also paid between $35 and $300 to join these organizations. But the phone calls of two to three hours were my greatest expense.

I tried to find people all over the country, with diverse backgrounds, diverse professions.

Sometimes I interviewed strangers I met on planes or trains or at parties. Sometimes I interviewed friends of friends. In fact, these interviews of friends of friends became more frequent as friends heard what I was doing and knew "just the right man for the book."

I certainly was pleased to interview this latter group because I knew their stories had to be true. After all, I could check them out with friends if I had to. As for the others, I believe they were, for the most part, telling their truths. Since many of the stories we tell about ourselves are only partially true, distorted by self-deception, and since we cannot have total self-knowledge or objectivity, I suspect that many of the tales must be taken with a grain of salt.

Why Did I Seek Out These Men?

Was I looking for a man for myself? Yes and no. Yes, I've been single for twenty-two years. I was married for twenty-seven years. We loved each other, but life threw too many curve balls at us. We separated and divorced. My husband died within six months of the divorce. I am the marrying type. I'm surprised that I've been single for so long. I did get engaged once, but my fiancé died.

I tell you these biographical details to help you understand my perspective. I did not intend this book to be scientific or encyclopedic. The sample is biased (mostly because it is limited to men who have paid money to join dating services). I am a college graduate with a Ph.D. in English Literature. I have three published books on my credit list and I've been a businesswoman, poet and professor. Naturally I gravitated to educated men, men of influence or creative men who have contributed or are still contributing to society. I tried to stay away from men with low self-esteem. Since I'm Jewish, there are more Jewish men in the mix as well.

I believe in monogamy, both inside and outside of marriage. I do **not** believe there is only one "right man" out there looking for me. I thought of my survey as a foray into the unknown. I tried to approach my subjects both with empathy and skepticism. Since I only met four of the men I found through dating services, I don't think that could be called "indiscriminate" seeking.

HOWEVER, I did meet one man over the phone whom I've traveled with for more than four years. He and I have a fine relationship, with love, respect and mutual admiration. I enjoy the cultural activities he enjoys, the same pleasures. My life has expanded enormously and I believe we are good for each other. I'll tell you about him in my first chapter, which includes his testimony, what he was looking for and what he found in me.

I like men. I like love stories. I like to hear about how boy meets girl, how boy gets girl, how girl meets boy and how she gets boy. But I also like the stories about how boy loses girl or girl loses boy.

I am limiting my stories to heterosexual males since these were the men I wanted to meet.

You should also be aware that for the sake of balance, I have included stories of several unsavory men who could be classified as undesirable and/or dangerous. Do not let these men frighten you. I want you to know they exist, so that you will have a healthy skepticism. As for the eccentrics, their stories were too good to be excluded. These men could be desirable for certain women who have their own, odd histories.

Freud and Chaucer: Their Relevance to Your Search

I am curious. I have read a lot of Freud and studied the British theories of object relationships. Freud, of course, threw up his hands and said, "What is it that women want?" I've concluded that Freud had never read Chaucer. It was time to answer Freud in the same spirit.

Like Freud, you also may not have read Chaucer. In brief, Chaucer was born in England in 1340 and died in 1400. He interviews, as I have, 29 people who tell tales to amuse each other on their religious pilgrimage to Canterbury Cathedral. The Wife of Bath was one of two women on the pilgrimage. Chaucer did have a comic eye for real people living in a common world. He and I both write with tongue in cheek, conveying our delight in God's creatures, even if some of them are eccentric, foolish or dangerous:

But Lord Christ, when it all comes back to me
remembering my youth and jollity
I had my world in my time.

It tickles me to the roots.
It does me good down to this very day
that while I could, I took my world and had my fling.

My Response to Freud: The Wife of Bath's Tale

Having been married five times to "worthy men," the Wife of Bath holds King Solomon up as a role model. She is a frank lady who tells all, that she married these men both for the money in their purses and the knowledge she could gain from them. She questions, "'Why at our creation were organs given us for generation?" Certainly not to remain virgins! In her prologue, she enumerates what she believes men want:

Some want us for our wealth, some for our figure,
Some want a woman who can dance, sing.
Some want kindness and some philandering.

But then, when they wed, all they do is complain and hide the keys to their chests. She tells us how she berated her husbands until they gave her what she wanted: sovereignty.

My dear, my own true wife,
Do as you will as long as you have life;
Preserve your honor and keep my estate.

Having explained what she wanted, she then tells the tale of a knight in Arthur's court who has raped a young maiden and who should be executed as a result of this action. However, the queen gives him back his life if he can come to the court in a year and tell her what "is the thing that most of all women desire." The knight meets a hag during the twelve-month journey who reveals the secret, but also makes him promise he will grant the next request she makes of him. The knight returns to the court and announces "women desire to have sovereignty and sit in rule and government above their husbands."

Suddenly, the old witch springs up and states the knight has gotten this secret from her and that he has pledged that he will grant her next wish.

"I wish you to marry me," she demands. The next day they marry, but the knight hides afterwards in the woods like an owl. Finally, he goes to her bed and looks at her ugliness. She tells him he has a choice between an ugly but faithful wife and a young and beautiful wife with whom he'll have to take his chances. The knight, having learned the secret well, says:

> My love and lady, my dear wife,
> In your wise government I put my life.
> I do not care;
> Choose either of the two.
> I am content,
> whatever pleases you.

Had Freud read Chaucer, he might have discovered that women and men have been in a perpetual state of struggle because of domination and control patterns that always revolve around who is on top. In our day, the issue has been equality.

I would be misrepresenting my findings if I told you that equality and control were the subjects talked about by most of my interviewees. But underlying a great many of their comments were echoes of this dilemma: who gets to be the dominant partner and who becomes the subservient one? Do older men want equality in marriage? I will return to this question after the 29 stories that follow.

The Variety of Men I Interviewed.

There are many ways to stereotype men (or women). The "rich man, poor man, beggar man and thief" classification is only relevant if it suggests the career of a person who becomes representative of his professional class (as in Chaucer). Certainly it is more interesting than the psychobable of labels about narcissism or sado-masochism or borderline personalities. I also tend to reject astrological labels about why you should choose a man who is compatible with your sign. If you're an Aries and he's a rat, watch out. If you're a monkey and he's a monkey, you'll get fleas. In the end, I borrow from Chaucer and use the profession of each man to describe his overall comic or tragic features and the range of his human characteristics.

Like Chaucer, I often take on the role of the narrator (hostess), granting each character (the interviewee) the liberty of telling his story. But I also tell tales that come out of my experience. These are told directly or disguised through a fictional character's voice. I am concerned about protecting the men I have known. Often, I change their professions, if their professions could reveal their identities. But I try not to distort their stories.

Of course, I also suffer from self-deception and personal bias. But I do not intend to seek revenge on any of my past male friends. As a writer, however, I cannot ignore the juicier parts of my own experiences and therefore, I admit to dramatization, irony and occasional hyperbole.

The interviewees are:

1. Jack, a political animal and dedicated dilettante, who tells our story.

II. Francis, a romantic, southern doctor.

III. Gregory, a recent widower, businessman and pillar of the community.

IV. Samson, a physician of preventive medicine.

V. Kevin, a judge with New Age propensities.

VI. John, an entrepreneur, who dashes about the world.

VII. Drake, a storyteller, who gets involved with Romeo and Juliet.

VIII. Hollis, an architect, whom I met in San Miguel de Allende (an idealist).

IX. Joe, a corporate executive, who believes in angels (an idealist).

X. Vincent, a black architect, with a vision of community (an idealist).

XI. Murray, a professor of oriental medicine, a screenplay writer and psychotherapist.

XII. Walter, a Watsu Practitioner (another Californian).

WHY YOU SHOULD NOT GIVE UP:
or HOW TO MODIFY YOUR EXPECTATIONS

In the course of my survey, I found stable, conscientious, hardworking, caring, sometimes romantic, sweet, helpful, curious, healthy men. They did not necessarily come in the shapes or sizes I wanted. But they do exist and they are looking for you. You might click. Many of you and many of them are good people who would probably like each other. Whether or not you would "fall in love" is a more complex question, based on unconscious determinables about your parents and siblings and past experiences.

My single women friends have complained: Single older men are dull, crude, rude, foolish, egocentric, infantile, unreliable, shallow, crazy, etc. They can't tolerate intimacy.

My answer is: Some are. But not all.

Many men I've interviewed say: The women I've dated are uninteresting, suburban, frivolous, vain, sexually rapacious, gold diggers, heart breakers, cold, rejecting, angry, ridiculing, takers.

My answer is: Some are. But some are not.

In the course of my research, I found many men whom I would love to call my friends. I also met my current romantic partner. If I had stayed at home, moaning and groaning that there was no one out there, none of this would have happened.

But as the song goes, "A Good Man Is Hard To Find." If you are shy or still hampered by the rules and paradigms of the fifties, depressed or full of fear, suffering from low self-esteem, you can still find someone who has his own limitations. He may not be a "good man," but he might be good enough.

I, too, went through a down period after my husband died. I was depressed. I had a lot to be depressed about. First, the doctor gave me uppers. I could not fall asleep. I threw them away. Then he gave me downers. I couldn't wake up. I threw them away. I cleared up my depression by swimming every day at the Watergate Health Spa. I had all the same feelings you may have had, you, my readers, who may feel hopeless, helpless, too old, too fat, and too unattractive, etc. After meeting men, I, too, would conclude, "there's no one out there for me."

BUT THEN I BEGAN KISSING FROGS

What made me do that? Lots of reasons, I suppose. Some of it came from the life force rising in me again. Some of it came from a healthy reaction to loneliness. Some of it came from a new perspective I was developing, thanks to the workshops I was attending and the books I was reading. Some of it came from the one rule I decided to follow: "Go with people who uplift my spirits. Stay away from people who drag me down."

But most of it came from my own intelligence which has always given me answers to dilemmas and painful situations. My father had always valued my mind. That was why he named me Minerva, the goddess of wisdom. Whatever sense of inferiority I had came from the facts that I was a poor, Jewish girl in a society that devalued second-best Avis qualities (in the thirties, forties and, also, in the fifties). But I did try harder and I was, for the most part, successful. Being single again at 50 was indeed a challenge. I knew I would have to change my sheltered life.

I have always loved diversity. I've never been afraid of the kindness of strangers and I've always enjoyed travel and adventures. I dated a lot as a teenager, had a good base for high self-esteem; I had dealt with a lot of demons in several years of analysis during my husband's illness. Although I was a romantic, I had a strong, realistic streak in me that kept me from believing: "There's only one man out there for me."

PERHAPS, YOU'VE DECIDED YOU'RE HAPPIER ALONE.

You have many friends and a rich social life. You have people to travel with. You have a family, children and grandchildren who want you to visit. You are doing creative work or volunteer work or you're still busy with paid employment. In your mind, your life is good enough. You're glad to be without the demands and adjustments of an intimate relationship. Then, by all means, don't read any further. If you are happy with your single life, that is absolutely fine.

BUT IF YOU WANT TO FIND SOMEONE, YOU CAN JOIN THE PILGRIMAGE.

There are thousands of available men. I'm not suggesting they are all wonderful. Some have serious idiosyncrasies and character flaws: cheaters, gigolos, emotional cripples who love only themselves, depressed men without any life force left, raging men who are repressing their anger, liars who aren't there for you. There are "bad" men whom you should not trust.

I don't dwell on this group. I simply include a few of them, along with the dangerous ones who gave me the willies.

I use that word *dangerous* without humor. The dangerous men were breakers of hearts, minds and spirit. They had been abused by mothers or fathers and relished being in pain or causing pain. They were in their sixties and seventies, sleeping with prostitutes who could give them AIDS. They had multiple partners. They are retired and think that the dearth of men gives them the right to play God's gift to older women. Beware! You can't tell these books by their covers. They might look like gentlemen. They might have taught at prestigious colleges, but when you open their books, you find Dorian Gray.

I have talked to many men who are NICE, but, unexciting or extremely shy. They can be good citizens, solid, responsible, and rational, but you have to be the one to supply the "juice," the""joie de vivre." They are moody or silent much of the time. They may blame women for their unhappiness. They are men who haven't stopped mourning for a dead or divorced spouse, a failed career, a lost childhood, and an unrealizable ideal.

As I've told you, I've given up the myth of one romantic'"right" man, a soul mate, a Heathcliffe, a nurturing mother-male. I, like many women who read Bronte and Austen, Flaubert and Tolstoy, spent years dreaming about meeting a kindred spirit, a male who would appreciate my soul. Or I tried to be the nurturing muse who sustained a creative, dynamic man who would become great, in part, because of my empathic devotion. That was the role held up to us by literature and by our history. In the fifties, the most influential book for my generation was "The Power of Sexual Surrender," by Marie Bonaparte. Women were naturally masochists. Childbirth required that we enjoy pain. We should enjoy self-sacrifice.

Thank God we evolved. We now understand and accept the values of friendship and complementary qualities. Thank God we've given up mergers. Thank God we've learned to include, rather than exclude all sorts of people whom we don't have to classify as potential mates, or the "one and only soul mate" of our one and only life. Bless these men I have interviewed for the insights they have provided into the wider human comedy. Bless them all. You can now find out for yourself whether any of the men I describe are worth your attention.

Before you begin reading these stories, if you are serious about wanting to find a man, look at the questionnaire in the appendix and fill it out. Then follow the directions about narrowing down your choices to find the most important qualities you want in a companion, a lover, a husband, and a friend.

I

"Variety in what is best is the joy of life."

— Baltasar Gracian

Jack, a former politician and a dedicated dilettante

Friends say to me, "You actually met him through a dating service? Why would a man like Jack join a dating service? He must know hundreds of women. He's such an attractive, intelligent, well-groomed and social man. There must be something wrong with him."

Jack loves to travel. Traveling is, in fact, his major passion. Since his divorce and his retirement from politics, he has spent most of his time seeing the world. He has a pad in Washington, DC and a condo in Naples, Florida. He still has many friends in the District and all over the U.S. But he was not finding the stimulation he wanted in Naples, Florida.

In the spring of 1998, he decided to visit Easter Island in the Pacific Ocean. He was looking for a new travel companion to go with him. That's why he joined "Single Adventurous Voyagers" to find such a person, a companion who would pay her own expenses. This seasoned traveler was not interested in going along with a person he did not know very well who would be financially dependent on him. At 73, he knew there were lots of interesting women who could and would pay for themselves.

When I read his profile and called him, he was in Washington, DC. Like my late husband, he was a lawyer who did not practice law. He had been passionate about politics and had worked on the Hill and served in the Ford White House. He loved cities, culture and new experiences. Having grown up in the small but wonderful town of Elmira, New York, to which he was still attached, he had even run for Congress as an Elmira native son. But he had become too citified in Washington, DC. Elmira did not elect him for Congress, but he did serve as an adviser to a President of the United States.

Jack's father had been a newspaper publisher and his mother was a strong, down-to-earth woman who coped well after her husband died. Jack came from a functional family. Unlike me, he had ancestors in the US who came here in the seventeenth century. He enjoyed his WASP status and was financially comfortable. He was pleased with himself and what he had accomplished.

1

His father's death, when he was fifteen, had marked him, mainly because he was an only child and his life changed significantly after that loss. But he did go to college and to law school and procured the jobs he wanted, because of his solid work ethic, his sense of purpose, his commitment to public service and his unshakable self-confidence.

I didn't learn all of this while interviewing him about his singlehood and his future desires. What I did learn that made me want to meet him was that we both shared a mutual friend, Ken Mansfield, who had been my late husband's good friend in the fifties.

"I like the way you interview," Jack said. "I've done my share of interviews, and I think you're first rate. I'd like to meet you," he continued. All this was said after an hour and a half of questions and answers.

"I love your deep, mellow voice," I responded. "I make it a rule not to meet the men I'm interviewing, but since we have a mutual friend, I think you're not likely to be an ax murderer. I'm retiring in a month and you do sound like a wonderful travel companion. I'd like to think about future trips after we get to know each other."

Then, we hit our first obstacle. He was traveling. I was traveling. When he was in the states, I wasn't and vice versa. He belonged to the Hemingway Society and was going to a conference in Les Saintes Maries de la Mer in the Camarques of France.

"I've planned a trip to Corsica," I replied, "from mid June till July 1."

"Unfortunately, I go to the Bohemian Grove in July for three weeks and then I'm scheduled to visit friends in Texas the first week in August."

"This is going to be difficult, since I go to Edinburgh for the Fringe Festival the second and third weeks in August."

"What about the fourth week in August?" he parried.

"That's fine. Why don't you come to Hartford," I answered.

So we met in Hartford after numerous phone calls and postcards. It wasn't love at first sight. It was love at second sight. He was wearing a hat that covered his face, a sort of sloppy Joe canvas affair that "old farts" wear. It was unbecoming. He also didn't smile (because he doesn't have wonderful teeth.). But during dinner he laughed a lot and when I was doing the dishes, he whirled me around and began to dance to the romantic music on the CD player. He danced me from room to room and I relaxed in his arms, happy that I had found a man who could do more than talk well. It's rare in my generation to find dancing men who are also intelligent and charming. I was to learn that behind this sense of rhythm lived a pre-verbal love of music that came out of his mind, fingers and toes spontaneously and deliciously without prompting.

I'll spare you the details of our day-to-day budding romance. The highlights are more important. At one point we went to Cape Cod, to my house in Truro. After dinner at my favorite restaurant, "The Martin House," Jack and I meandered around Provincetown and we popped into a shop, which sold pheasant boas. I tried one on and pranced about, knowing that I would never buy such a thing. First of all, they were expensive and, second, I am not the boa type. I'm more of a Pendleton suit woman who's become artistic. I don't wear sexy clothing. I wear comfortable, folkish dresses or black slacks and colorful shirts.

The next week I had to fly to San Francisco and a week later I returned to Hartford. A long skinny box was waiting for me. I opened it up and there was the boa with a note from Jack. "To keep you warm until I see you again."

That did it, along with the singing and dancing on my deck at the Cape in the moonlight under a sky of structured, orderly stars. All was right in the heavens and in my own little space on earth.

One of the best surprises was that Jack was an addictive reader. Even though he had spent a life in Washington politics, he had deep interests in literature, in history, in art, in film, in drama and in music. He had played in a combo as a drummer in high school and knew everything there was to know about jazz and jazz musicians. His favorite place and time was when Hemingway and Fitzgerald and all the literati hung out as expatriates in Paris.

All of this contributed to our mutual attraction, since I too loved Paris and had lived there for a year in 1952. It was my favorite city.

Not only was Jack an art collector, not only had he studied acting, not only was he a film aficionado, but also he was a voracious reader with whom I could share books. That was almost as difficult to find as a man who could dance and sing my songs. I remember being on a train with a former boyfriend, Ernie, wanting to read my book. Ernie didn't read. He was an artist, a graphic artist, but he didn't read anything but newspapers.

I never realized how much the reading habit can separate people. Having the same interests does make a huge difference, because after the initial flurry

3

of stories about your life and mine and the daily talk of preferences in food and drink and activity, there rises a hunger to be with and yet be alone, absorbed in a good book. Jack understood that hunger and satisfied it frequently.

Later in our relationship, he took me to Naples, Florida where we spent a blissful week walking on the beach, eating healthy meals and reading, reading, reading.

But I'm getting ahead of our story. In the fall of 1998 we met each other every weekend: in New York, in Toronto, in Asheville, North Carolina, in Washington, DC, in Boston, and for Christmas, in Anguilla. I rented a small villa in Anguilla and Jack and my son and I had a delightful ten days. It was a new and wonderful experience for me since Jack is Episcopalian and I am Jewish. We celebrated both holidays with lots of gifts, and midnight mass at a local church that had a saxophone player and twenty Anguillian choir members. Since Jack loves gourmet food as much as I do, he adored the restaurants.

Jack writes a yearly newsletter to his many friends in which he mentions the best restaurants he's gone to, the best films he's viewed, the best plays he's seen, the best books he's read, etc. Friends tease him that it takes them months to read and digest his suggestions. He includes a section of commentary and predictions.

All in all I find it a fascinating letter, one that is both thoughtful and useful. He keeps track of everything that's worthwhile in his daytimer notebook. Since he's been retired for almost 21 years, this kind of discipline helps structure his life, along with his contributions to his favorite organization, the Bohemian Club.

"I've never heard about the Bohemian Club," I confessed.

"Well, you've said I'm an elitist. I suppose the Bohemian Club is my most elitist activity. I waited 17 years to get in. It used to be a club for bohemians in San Francisco: artists, musicians, writers, etc. But they began to let in people who were rich when they realized they needed money to do the things they wanted to do."

"And what do they do?" I asked naively.

"Well, they have a three week encampment in the woods every summer. They put on musicals, listen to lectures, learn about what's going on that's new in the world, politically, economically, scientifically, culturally. There's a lot of male camaraderie and good feelings. "

"Did you get in as a bohemian or a rich man?"

"They also let in men who've been influential. When I was on the White House staff, I did have some influence."

Since I had been the first chairperson of the Permanent Commission on the Status of Women in Connecticut, I wasn't thrilled that Jack belonged to an organization that excluded women. But I realized that Jack was not a typical male who excluded women out of fear or sexism. He respected my intellect and seemed to admire my strength. He treated me as an equal, as indeed I was.

Even rarer than a dancer, a singer and a lover of literature, it was practically impossible to hook up with a man over 60 who wanted to find a woman who was an equal. That was not necessarily the norm when I was growing up. And Jack was seven years older than I was. Fortunately he had a daughter who was the mother of two children but she had carved out a professional life and was also managing one of his buildings in Washington, DC. He was exceedingly proud of her.

In January of 1999, I took Jack with me to my favorite spa, Rancho La Puerta, in Northern Mexico. I had been going there for years. I have taught a poetry workshop at The Ranch and I could bring a guest with me. It's a place I love and I was eager to share it with him. He had never been to a spa and I wasn't sure he would like it. The first day he took an exercise class called "pilates." It's a class that works on posture and abdominals. The instructor asked the students,

"What does an arched back remind you of?"

"Ecstasy!" shouted Jack.

After that I couldn't keep the women away from him. First, the ratio of women to men is about 15 to 1. Second, Jack is a live one. I watched him enjoy himself beyond measure. But I finally said, "You're here as my guest. Please come back on your own if you want all this attention."

I must confess that I was jealous of all those blondes who were flirting with him. One woman actually asked him for his phone number in DC right in front of me. I had a similar experience in Toronto where I took Jack for his first Bar Mitzvah. While I was in the ladies' room, a widow in front of him in the synagogue tried to make a "connection." Luckily I got back in time to extricate him.

Jack has since been back to the Ranch and he and I are more of a couple. In fact, everyone thinks we are married. The Ranch is special because, unlike other spas, there are interesting programs that stimulate the mind, as well as the body and spirit. We have both felt fulfilled by being there and hope that our visits continue.

After Rancho la Puerta, we went to San Miguel de Allende, a town in the mountains north of Mexico City in the state of Guanajuato. We were so happy in San Miguel that we returned for a second and a third year. The second year we rented a house and friends and family came to visit. Yet another paradise! Recently we bought a small condo together in this delightful town and we look forward to spending many winters there.

It isn't anything I had planned to do. But I realize it opens up a whole new opportunity to enjoy new, interesting people and to expand my life with a new language, a new culture, and a new community. "Make it new" is probably my battle cry, a way of expressing the creative life force that always wants to give birth to a brand new being. I've met a Mexican family that feels like my own. They've visited me at the Cape. I have the strangest feeling of closeness with them, as though we were meant to have met each other.

Our list of trips now includes an Elderhostel to Costa Rica, the Edinburgh Fringe Festival, and parts of France, Spain, Italy, Germany, Austria and England. We "did" South America (Peru, Argentina and Brazil) and a Baltic cruise that gave us a bird's eye view of St. Petersburg and four Scandinavian capitals. We're planning future trips to China, Bali, and other countries in the Far East.

In the year 2000, Jack celebrated his seventy-fifth birthday. He decided to have many parties in different parts of the country so that he could see all of his friends and have a sentimental journey. There are few people in this world who love parties as much as Jack does and who are still in touch with their roots and the people they grew up with. The first of the six parties was in Naples, Florida and the last was in Venice, Italy. They were all great fun and quite different.

Jack says that the Venetian party was so fulfilling, he will have another one there when he reaches 80.

I am not trying to make you envious, my readers. What I want you to conclude from all this is:

THIS CAN HAPPEN TO YOU.

I want you to read what Jack has to say about how it all happened, what he wanted and what he has found. Then I'll come back and give you some suggestions of what worked for us.

Jack's point of view:

"BE CAREFUL WHAT YOU WISH FOR; YOU MAY GET IT." All of us have heard that cautionary saying and some have regretted their wishes when the wishes have come true. My story is the opposite.

In 1997, in the wake of a failed romance, I considered trying to find my next relationship via the advertising route. I sketched my proposed "In search of" entry:

> *Single, solvent, sensuous, social senior seeks Seven*
> *Sisters sort for shared socializing and sojourning.*

The words were carefully chosen to convey my message: that I was over 65, self-supporting, interested in the pleasures of art, reading, food, touching, music, theater, etc., and that I enjoyed meeting people and a good party. My ideal woman would be a college graduate, preferably from one of the quality women's schools in New England. I wanted both a social and travel companion. The choice of alliteration was simply an attention grabber.

I will never know what results that proposal would have produced, since I never placed it. One reason was that I move around a lot and I didn't know which medium would be best. I base myself in Washington, DC where I had a 30-year career but I also spend time in Florida and part of the summer in California. The rest of the time I'm traveling. Primarily I was seeking a travel companion, and if it developed that we loved each other, so much the better.

Fast forward to January 1998, when I decided to go to Chile and Easter Island in March. Unable to find a friend who was interested, I came upon a travel publication which mentioned an exchange service for those seeking travel companions. I joined, paying a fee by credit card. Soon I received a profile form to fill in, listing age, education, religion, past travel, future travel, likes and dislikes, financial preference, etc. Along with the form came condensed profiles of women who were members already. I requested full profiles of five women who looked promising (one even specified Easter Island), but nothing came of these contacts. "Travel plans already in place."

"Just found a new boyfriend." "Just had a hip replacement." These were typical responses.

I finally decided to drop my outreach and go alone.

By the end of April, I was back in Washington, DC and I had decided to stay in that evening. My phone rang and a pleasant woman's voice announced that she was Minerva and that she had obtained my profile from "Single Adventurous Voyageurs" and that she was researching for a book on single men over sixty. She asked if I would consent to a lengthy telephone interview. I could have declined and ended the contact, but there was a persuasive, intelligent quality in her voice and I agreed to the interview. It was one of those decisions that changes a life.

More than an hour later, I had told her a great deal about myself. She was an excellent interviewer and I told her so. I also suggested that we meet. I had done a great deal of interviewing myself and admired her ability to get so much personal information out of me in so short a time. In addition, I found out she was a graduate of Smith College, one of the Seven Sister colleges I respected. I also learned that she was approaching retirement from her university position and wanted to increase her traveling. It seemed that out of nowhere, the woman of my never-published advertisement had called me.

Our eventual meeting four months later in Hartford confirmed for me that my wishes had been answered. After another visit to Cape Cod, we were soon planning our joint sojourning. Nearly three years later, our pattern seems to be set: three to four weeks at her Cape House in the summer and fall, about the same time at my Florida beach place in the winter and spring, occasional weekends in Washington, New York, Toronto or at other friends' houses, two and a half months in Mexico in the winter, plus two or three grand visits to Europe, Asia or South America in the Spring and Fall. Each time we go away together for more than two weeks, we spend at least two weeks apart to catch up on mail, taxes, social, charitable and family obligations. This break helps Minerva finish the writing that she's working on and both of us to build up some anticipation for our next exciting journey.

Why has it worked so far? Despite a good many differences in family background, religion and politics, we complement each other and share many characteristics. We both are highly friend-oriented and have scores of close friends around the country (and some abroad). Most important, I like her friends and she likes mine. Together we also have made new friends on our many travels. We both love art, movies, good eating (a pitfall for both of us), parties (informal with a variety of interesting people), good reading, theater, jazz and other types of music, political discussions, and, of course, travel. We can both be experimental and adjust to many kinds of circumstances.

Minerva is more intellectual than I. I am more practical than she (in some ways). As a poet, she often thinks in metaphors, whereas I think in facts. These characteristics balance each other and make for a stimulating relationship.

By coincidence we are economically balanced, with roughly the same amount of assets and income. When she is in my homes, she is my guest; when I am in hers, I am her guest. On travels, we share expenses and we each tip what we wish. Though I have at times argued against her impulse to buy a big ticket item (on the grounds of practicality), we do not argue about money because it is either her decision or mine whether to spend our own.

Does all this sound too idyllic? Perhaps! But it has proved to be remarkably easy to reach with a compromise here, a stated preference there and overlying it all, acceptance that we are equal partners in a loving combination that we both know we are lucky to have found. Obviously we each have had to be flexible in many things and tolerant of the other's quirks and foibles. These attitudes have come with maturity and age.

Although we communicate very well, we both value silence and some solitude, even when we are together. Therefore there is no need for constant chatter just to fill the air with syllables (a failure of several women in my past). Finally, there's that ineffable element, good chemistry, which underlies all our activities and emotions and lubricates possible rough spots.

To sum up, my advice to the reader is: wish for what you want, be realistic in your expectations, and you may be surprised at the good results, sometimes from an unlikely quarter.

It worked for Minerva and me. We are happy. May it work for you as well.

II

"Age doesn't protect you from love,
but love, to some extent, protects you from age."

— Jeanne Moreau

Francis: a true romantic doctor

Francis is 67. He is six feet tall, weighs 185 pounds. His picture reveals a high forehead, white hair and twinkling, seductive eyes. His smile is absolutely riveting. What a wonderful, warm man, I think. All of this is evident in the photograph he has included in his "Single Adventurous Voyager" profile.

He tells me over the phone that his first wife died of ovarian cancer. He has lost his second wife to lung cancer. He confesses that he met his second wife through a dating service. That answers my question: Why should a man like you join a dating service? If he found one wife through such a service, why not another? The second wife had been married to a writer. Her first husband had written seven best sellers. He had died and she raised the children by herself. She was well traveled, very beautiful, and extremely intelligent.

His first wife was very intelligent also. She could do anything, he insisted. "She had an IQ of 160. She picked up information so quickly that she learned to use a computer in one week and got a job as a computer programmer." I felt his pride and his loss. Imagine losing two wives to cancer. It was Valentine's Day, just five years ago that his second wife passed away. Now he is looking for a woman between 45 and 60.

He has been a widower for five years and doesn't like it. He can cook and do domestic chores, but he would rather have a wife take care of that part of his life.

Cancer seems to have become the nemesis in all of his relationships. The woman he's been dating has a son with lymphatic cancer. This woman barely has time for him. "She likes to talk to me on the phone a great deal. I'm a doctor and I've had a lot of experience with cancer."

I was beginning to feel terrible. What a sad life. What sad stories. But then he begins to tell me about his interests beyond his medical practice as a family practitioner. He has published many books, one about controlling your weight and another, a children's' book, especially for his seven grandchildren. He had three children from his first marriage.

Finally I ask," If you could choose a person for this stage in your life who could be exactly the person you want, what would she be like?"

"Another soul mate," he answers.""I'm not looking for a trophy. Sure there are young nurses on the fourth floor who flirt with me. But I am not interested in cute young things."

The closest he could come to defining HER is that she should have a certain spark.""I remember sitting at a counter in an airport and a woman came to have lunch, a cheese sandwich. Suddenly I was aware of this woman. I'll never forget her face. A bell went off. I can still hear it. Somehow I felt connected to her. I think that's the way it's going to happen again."

No question about it, I was talking to a romantic. "Across a crowded room" he would see a stranger. However, when I ask him about negatives, what might turn him off, he knows right away that he couldn't marry an antisocial person. He is a social animal. Any future wife would have to be someone who likes people and is liked by them.

Also he avoids women who are too domineering He can't stand women who are so busy talking, they pay no attention to him. He is a bit of a homebody. "I'm pretty traditional, I guess," he states. " Some women might find me egotistical. But I'm very caring."

Yes, he is looking for a woman between 40 and 60, even though he is 67. But my overall reaction to Frances is highly positive. His story belies the concept that people get what they deserve, that they attract people with the same vibes and states of awareness. Francis' story seems to me closer to that of Job, who could not understand why he was made to suffer.

For me, the only problem was where Francis lived, in a southern state, far from the cultural and intellectual centers of the East. The politicians of his state are rather reactionary. Perhaps this isn't a problem for you. I have heard of matches that have been successful, despite the fact that individuals lived far away geographically. But the days of"'whither thou goest' I will go" are over for me! You, however, might be happy commuting or moving to his territory.

I must confess I fell in love with a man who lived five blocks away from me. It was a devastating romance. He was a widower and I thought I knew him well. He thought he knew me because we had been social friends for many years. We had similar backgrounds, mutual friends, the same religion, and the same kind of educational background.

As it turned out, we didn't know each other at all. We were from two different continents with two different ways of thinking and being. Physical proximity only helped us discover how little we had in common. It turned out that he wanted to replace his wife ASAP. He was not like Francis who had been alone for five years.

I learned a lot from this relationship, rules which Francis already knows:

Rule 1) Don't marry a widower (or widow) who is excessively dependent.

Rule 2) Don't marry a man (or woman) who is looking for a duplicate of a dead spouse.

Rule 3) Don't give your heart away to someone ruled by the preferences of his grown-up children.

Rule 4) Don't imagine that a seventy-five year old man who's been taken care of is going to put your needs first.

I have a friend named Grace who was my roommate in Paris. She fell in love with a man who is a recent widower. She told me her story which illustrates all the points I've just made, and proves that *propinquity* is **not** an all-important factor.

III

Grace's tale about Gregory, a business man and a pillar of the community in which they lived.

"Minerva, I know you'll want to include my latest romance in your book about single men over 60. I don't think you ever met Gregory when you came to Chicago. We grew up together in Evanston. Greg and his wife, Heather, were social friends for years and years. In fact, Gregory and Jacob were golf buddies. Greg and Heather belonged to our country club and we had dinner with them frequently. When Jacob died, Heather still included me in her Christmas party, something that didn't happen with other friends, threatened by my singlehood.

I was sad when I learned that Heather had breast cancer. She was a fighter and a brave woman. She took the chemo treatments well and she looked great in a wig and later with a short-cropped hairdo. She had lived for five years after her first episode and we all thought she was free and clear. But then it came back. Gregory was an exemplary husband and stayed by her side, not like some husbands who can't stand to watch their wives sicken.

When she died, it was somewhat of a relief. It had taken two years before she progressed to the worst stage, bedridden and incontinent. After her death, Gregory told everyone he did not want to be alone at home in their large house. He would prefer lots of invitations for dinner. Women began calling him immediately, asking him to concerts, dinners and local events. Gregory was still good-looking, relatively well off and reliable.

Even though I was a long-time friend of Gregory and his late wife, I missed the funeral because I was away. I had been a widow for almost ten years. I knew what it was like to reach over and find no one there, to feel the silence of a house that no longer comforts you, to be perpetually cold, lost, unprotected, without the one who had been everything to you for twenty years.

So I called Gregory and invited him to dinner. It was a snowy night in March. The other couple whom I also invited canceled at the last moment and Gregory and I dined alone. He poured out his heart, telling me all the details of Heather's death, how she fell in the bathroom, how he had to call someone because he wasn't strong enough to move her body away from the door, how his children had been taking care of him since her death, how he hated being alone, how he was trying to adjust, putting on a happy face.

And then he started to cry. I put my arms around him and rocked him like an infant. I guess he liked that. When he left, he said he wanted to see more of me. He'd be back.

And so it started, our romance.

Gregory was terribly lonely and I was tired of being a widow. Gregory and I had known each other for forty years. I remembered him when he was a good-looking athlete in high school and a handsome soldier who went off to fight in World War II. I remembered his parents. I knew his four children. In fact, our kids had gone to the same schools. I knew him to be social, gregarious, warm and loving. He was a model father and husband and he served on as many boards as Jacob had. My husband had been more handsome, bright, and charismatic. But the biggest difference between Greg and Heather and Jacob and me was that we were more "culturally and intellectually" involved.

Loneliness and sexual starvation and propinquity were perhaps the three strongest components of my attraction. But for Gregory, there was his flaming need to replace Heather ASAP.

Gregory soon discovered that he was fascinated by my intellect and experience. To Gregory, I was an exciting, exotic flower, more unconventional than Heather. I had traveled abroad during the last ten years, had friends all over the world, lived in Spain and spoke Spanish fluently. I had quit the country club soon after Jacob died. I didn't want to hang out with the same people who had known each other forever. I had never enjoyed that membership. I went to the club because it was good for Jacob's business.

Six months after Heather's death, Greg asked me to marry him. He actually got down on his knees and said, "I know what a good mother you've been. You and Heather were alike in that way. And I know what a caring person you are. You've taken care of me when I've been sick in the last six months. You've brought me back to life. I know that being with you is exciting, challenging. You have the qualities that Heather lacked. You have deep intellectual curiosity. You are a painter. You even read poetry. Even though I'm color blind, you've already taught me how to look at paintings and understand them without focusing on the colors. You make me happy. I love you and I want you to be my wife."

His words were sweet and I needed to hear them. I immediately said yes and told my family I was going to get married again. Greg told his family and all hell broke loose. One of his daughters was dependent on Greg financially and when he told her we would have a pre-nuptial agreement and preserve all his assets for his children, she relented. The others were shocked that he was acting so precipitously, that he was insulting the memory of his dead wife who hadn't been in the grave for a full year. They were dependent on him emotionally and insisted that he keep the engagement a secret, for the sake of propriety.

I decided that we should go away for a weekend and think through these reactions. I invited Greg to my summerhouse in the Indiana Dunes, south of Chicago. This is a special place where I can paint and meditate. Greg had parents who always went to Cape Cod where they had a house in Eastham. He had summered there throughout his childhood in a fairly modest cottage that was cheek-to-jowl with other cottages. Even though he grew up in Evanston, he had never been to the Dunes.

At the last moment I included another couple, whom I wanted Greg to meet. In retrospect, I see I also wanted to get their take on Greg, to see what they thought about Greg and me getting married.

Mortimer was an academic, a Yeats scholar. Greg said he wanted to meet my friends who were more intellectual than his friends. He was tired of knowing only lawyers and doctors and businessmen.

But Gregory was surprised when he got to my house which stood all alone on a hill of sand. There were open spaces and infrequent houses. Neighbors were there, but at a distance.

"In my old beach colony in Eastham, you can reach out and touch your neighbor's house. Compared to my beach neighborhood, this looks like wilderness," said Greg, puzzled by the pioneer woman he was planning to marry.

"It's hardly wilderness living. I have three bathrooms, a washer and dryer and a dishwasher. I have several good neighbors, a potter, a painter, and a university vice president," I said.

Mortimer and Mary, my guests for the weekend, suddenly appeared in their modest gray Dodge. They were carrying bundles of fruits and vegetables from their garden. I love to entertain this couple. They adore my house and Mary always cooks marvelous food. Mortimer is my best intellectual buddy. We know each other exceedingly well.

Since it was late, everyone ate and went to bed. The next morning Greg woke at 7:30 A.M. He had the habit of waking very early, eating a bowl of cereal and a banana and reading the newspaper cover to cover. That morning he followed his usual pattern, but so did Mort, who was also an early riser. I was not. I slept till nine and greeted Greg cheerfully.

"Hi, honey. How are you today? Did you sleep well?"

Greg did not respond. He glanced at me sullenly and went back to his paper. All morning he buried his nose in the newspaper. Even when we went walking, Greg was silent. I pleaded with him.

"What is wrong, Greggy? Are you ill? Have I done anything wrong? Did your children call? Is there anything wrong with them? Tell me. I've never seen you like this."

Finally, Greg whined, "Mort ate my banana."

"Well, couldn't you go to Beverly Shores and get another banana?" I asked.

"That's not the point," Gregory shouted. "I don't like your friends. They are totally inconsiderate. Couldn't he have asked me? Couldn't he have offered me half of the banana?"

I was astonished at this regression. Greggy was, after all, seventy years old. I suddenly had a few flashbacks from the past months. I remembered a few incidents of compulsive behavior. Greg couldn't mail a letter. His wife had to drop all letters in the mailbox. He could not go to the cleaners. His wife had to go to the cleaners. He did not and could not eat lobsters unless someone else opened the shells. And then there was the night the electricity went off. He would not touch the fuse box. He made me do it.

"Hey," Mort called. "Is everything all right?"

Mort had noticed that I was looking quite puzzled and sad.

"Everything is fine!" I shouted to Mort and Mary who were examining some bird and animal tracks. We were taking a walk amongst the shrub oaks. We weren't swimming because Gregory was used to chlorinated pools, not large, fresh water lakes.

Gregory had lapsed into silence again and I began thinking about certain facts. Greg had laughed all through the "English Patient," because there were many costume changes. Greg didn't recognize characters from one frame to the next. He didn't like going to museums because he was colorblind. Nor did he read anything but biographies of political men. I had to teach him how to read the simplest poem. He had a heart attack several years ago. Was he really as healthy as he said he was? I had taken him to a yoga retreat, for his arthritis. He was so disoriented, that we left the next day. He particularly complained about the lights. The grounds at night seemed dark and threatening.

But most of all, I went over all the difficulties Gregory was having with his grown children. They were in their forties, after all. He accepted their control over him. One of them had mentioned to her father that there was no reason to marry me. People can live together unmarried, now, without disgrace.

By the time we returned to the house for lunch, I was full of doubts about marrying. Then Mort asked a seemingly innocent question. "Grace, since you and Greg are engaged, where is your ring?"

Gregory hit the ceiling. "It's none of your business," he shouted.

I was ashamed of him. Mort looked taken aback and Mary suggested that they leave. I insisted that they stay and Gregory went to our room to take a nap.

That night I turned to Gregory in bed and said, "You know I love you. But I'm not so sure about getting married. You are having a hell of a time with your children and I know they have some justification for their opposition. It's awfully soon after your wife's death. Maybe it's best if we just stay unmarried."

"No! It wouldn't be right. We live in a town where everyone would gossip," Greg responded.

"I care about the gossip, but that determines very little," I continued. "For me, the bottom line is: Do you truly love me?"

"Well, love is a transitory emotion," he answered in a cold voice.

I hopped out of bed and raced into the adjoining room and locked the door. How could I have been so stupid? How could I have gotten myself into this ridiculous situation? I who believed that love was forever; true love was forever. How could I have been so blind, not to see that this man was wrong for me? What should I do? Should I ask him to leave? Would he have another heart attack? After all, he was an old friend. After all, we had been so intimate. I had nursed him when he had the flu. I knew he was a lightweight intellectually. But, we had many nights of laughter and forgetting. I know his secrets. He knows mine.

I fell asleep crying, feeling the sadness more than the anger.

The next day Gregory left. Mort and Mary were still there. I told Mort about the banana story. Mort doubled over with laughter.

" I hate to say it, but you're well rid of him. What an infant. And let's face it, Grace. He wasn't worth your little finger. You were too different from each other. What kind of a life would you have had? Did you want to belong to his Country Club? From what you've told me, his kids would have driven you nuts. You would be at the bottom of the heap in his affections. You think you'd ever have time to read or paint again? You'd be busy picking lobster out of the shell.

"Thank God, he's gone. Thank God, you're free again to be who you are. Metaphorically you are a mountain climber. He is a low-lander who won't leave his provincial nest. What a relief."

I knew Mort was right. In a few months, Gregory met another woman just like his wife. She also had oodles of money. He married her after six or seven dates. I've gone on to live my life.

MORAL OF GRACE'S TALE

Grace was actually lucky. Lots of women and men whose spouses die do rush into marriages and relationships too quickly because they are lonely or because they think they know the other person, or even because the sex is good.

More Rules:

Rule 5)   Just because the sex is good, don't rush into marriage.

Rule 6)   Avoid people who are full of fear or creatures of habit. (unless you are full of fear or a creature of habit.)

Rule 7)   Don't deny what you perceive. (Grace saw all of Greg's weaknesses, but chose to put on her rosy glasses).

Now look at the questionnaire in the appendix. Which qualities in Gregory and Francis appealed to you. OBVIOUSLY, they are both romantics, sensitive, heart-centered, tender, caring, kind, sexy, passionate, intelligent, charming, etc. But one is more conventional and main stream. The other is playful and more fantasy ridden. Which one do your prefer? Is kindness high on your list? If it is, you would choose Francis over Gregory.

IV

*"So now I go beyond these clichés of plenty and paradise
to a place where there are fewer lies."*
– *Angel Tongues and Lobster Tales*
– Minerva H. Neiditz

Samson: a physician who knows himself

The next man I interviewed was a doctor, but he represented a newer type of "modern medicine." He was a doctor of alternative medicine. His voice on the phone was energetic and deep. He did not include a photo in his profile from "The Best and the Brightest." He sounded confident. He was frightfully busy, he told me, but he would talk to me the following Monday at 3:30 p.m.

I called him back on that Monday and told him my bias. I needed to find some men to illustrate that widows and divorcees of a certain age don't have to stay at home alone. He said I might change my mind after interviewing him when I learned that he had three wives. He had married the first wife when he was very young. The main reason they had divorced was that she did not want to have children, and he did.

"My dad was crazy about her. He has kept her in the family, inviting her to all family functions."

The second wife was naturally someone whom he thought would make a great mother. She was that, but the marriage petered out after thirteen years. They did have two children and the fact that they got divorced did not traumatize the kids. He told me he moved two minutes away by car.

Again, his father included the second wife in all family get-togethers.

The third wife was not so fortunate. He characterized her as difficult and challenging. He was in the middle of a divorce. Even though he had lived alone for almost nine years, he had made a bad choice. In fact, he felt his last marriage had been a disaster. He did try to sound positive with statements about: "I was committed to her, even though she was very difficult." He spoke vaguely about her verbal abuse and the fact that she wouldn't move out of the house. They had to continue speaking to each other.

"It has taught me patience and flexibility, " he insisted.

I am somewhat suspicious of people who find something positive in every situation. Like Pangloss who lives in the best of all possible worlds, they seem to court disaster. I can't think of anything worse than living in the same house with someone who hates you, but won't leave because she would lose her status and suffer legal consequences. He had been in that situation for 14 months. My heart went out to both of them. Even though the divorce wasn't final, Samson had started dating. He said he had a "war" test. If he mentioned the "war" and his date assumed it was Vietnam rather than World War II, then this person was too young for him.

"I'm looking for a high achiever, a woman with her own career, a woman who loves her work as I love mine. I don't want more children. I've done that, been there. The baths, the 2 AM. feedings. The Saturday outings."

When he talked about his macro schedule, I understood why he wanted a working wife, absorbed in her own career. In the winter he taught skiing for a month. In the summer he participated in the racing sport of triathlon.

In addition, he was interested in politics, culture, travel and other sports. I also understood why he had joined a dating service. Location, again, was a bit of a problem. He lived near, but not in a large metropolitan city. Often the women had to come quite far to see him. A woman with a full-time career might have preferred his coming to see her. If she were younger and wanted babies, that was definitely out.

But the main problem was his absolute requirement that the woman be "non-ego-based."

When I asked him what he meant by that, he said," That means she should be able to depersonalize, not take things personally. She has to understand and practice a cognitive approach—see us as a team— never act unilaterally—always take my views into consideration."

"I've met many women who say they want a committed relationship. They talk the talk, but don't walk the walk," he summarized. I thought about his requirement. I had dated a man who told me he and his wife used to settle their problems by sitting in a bathtub together. They would take turns expressing their feelings. They each timed themselves for five minutes. Then the other took a turn. The purpose was to defuse anger and arrive at rational responses. But the sitz bath formula didn't work. Why? Because his wife finally declared that she was going to leave him. She went off with a lesbian.

While Samson was talking about women who break their agreements, I stared at his profile page from "The Best and the Brightest." One of the most provocative questions was: Describe what you consider to be a perfect Sunday.

Samson began by saying that a perfect Sunday was impossible to achieve (since perfection is impossible to achieve and perfectionist striving is ultimately destructive). He then included a copious list of possibilities: some great sex, good workout, yard work, watching sports on TV, going to a museum, a matinee, or a movie in the evening, time with family, a really good meal, skiing or racing, etc.

His answers to the questions on the profile were candid and well written. Here is another example: The traits he was seeking in a partner/companion were <u>honesty,</u> integrity, high ethical standards of personal and social behavior, intelligence, humor, easygoingness, really good looks, happy with self and life, adventuresome, career success and satisfaction, sexiness, style, calmness and sanity. No ambivalence about the relationship, open, the same or similar politics, supportive emotionally, etc.".

One might conclude that he was straightforward, saying exactly what he wanted. I, however, noticed a tone that sounded pompous, patronizing and a bit pedantic ("First let me tell you that since perfection is impossible.").

I said, " It sounds as though you are a positive thinker, a man who values health above all. You have a balanced life. But do you have a dark side?"

" Some women tell me I'm too good to be true," he replied.

Later he called me back and said candidly.""I have been accused of suffering from the three P's: Pomposity, Pedantry and Patronization."

I suddenly felt I was talking to a very honest man, one who was able to see his own flaws. He has tons of energy, is curious and articulate, balanced and passionate about his interests.

"Samson, you don't seem to be a once-and-forever romantic. You're very realistic and clear about what kind of a person you want to be with."

"You're right. I'm not a romantic. I know too much about fatal attractions. I see a lot of people who fool themselves into illusionary ecstasy. It's a big part of New Age blindness that love is all you need, that you can arrive at the heavenly gates through sexuality.

"I have a good friend, a judge, someone I grew up with, who is Catholic and still married, but he's bored with his wife. All she does is shop and take care of her grandchildren. He's still virile and good-looking. He stays up all night meditating, going inside and exploring his inner life. He is a full-fledged romantic like his father, an Irish sea captain and mystic. Kevin is studying to be a hypnotist. He's a great storyteller. He has the gift of gab from his mother. She didn't give up on him when the doctors said he wouldn't live."

"This sounds like it's going to be a great story for my book. Please go on."

"I'll tell you his story because I know it will help your readers, but you must understand that I've changed the names, locations, everything. And Kevin is not a patient. He's a friend."

By the way, in a recent survey done for the AARP (*Dating and Romance: A Study of Midlife Singles,* by Knowledge Networks, Inc.), one conclusion reached is that divorced men are the most likely candidates for remarriage.

V

"Old men ought to be explorers."

– T.S. Eliot

Samson's tale about Kevin, the Judge and his lover, Kiki

"Kevin loves to go to conferences and retreats. His wife has left him to be with her family in New York. Kevin goes to a new age retreat called Kripalu where you learn to do yoga. He meets a woman who is divorced, an older woman about 60, who has had a rough time of it. He thinks he's fallen in love with her. He told her that he and his wife have separated.

In a way of speaking, it's true. The wife doesn't want him anymore as a lover. He eats his meals out. She won't cook for him. He goes to McDonald's for breakfast. Kevin takes good care of himself. He is on a good regimen, except for McDonald's. He takes two exercise classes a day. He eats abstemiously. And Kiki, the new woman, is a bit plump, he tells me. At first, he was trying to help her with her weight problem. When they returned to the city, after talking at Kripalu, he asked her out. They ate fruit salad and went to the movies every night. They both love movies and Kiki's pattern is to eat too much at night.

That all sounds pretty innocent, doesn't it? But last week they went to bed and the inevitable happened. It was all so wonderful for both of them that Kevin didn't go to work for five days. They literally didn't leave the house for seven days. He told me it was like being God and creating the earth. They made love and sang songs and he told her tales and she told him tales and they bonded completely: mind, body and spirit. Nothing like this had ever happened to them before.

Kevin is a good-looking man with broad shoulders and a playful disposition. His eyes sparkle. He can be a lot of fun. He's very sensuous and probably a wonderful lover. Kiki is beautiful, he says, with large bosoms like his mother's and black hair and green eyes. She's plump but very attractive and curvaceous. She's been alone for quite a while. Her husband left her and she hasn't been with a man for many years. She is, apparently, completely and madly in love with Kevin. He's having the time of his life making this lady happy. Kevin has a lot of optimistic, unrealistic ideas."

"What are his ideas?" I interjected. I was certainly spellbound at the image of two people over sixty in bed for seven days and nights. I wondered when they found time for meals. But I didn't want to interrupt Samson's flow.

"He thinks the mind controls the body so much that if you feed the mind desirable images, you can change all the bad scripts you've grown up with. This is not a new idea. The hypnotist, Erickson, I think, used this as the basis for his practice. Kevin is learning how to do this himself. He used to be very heavy. He feeds himself images of rotten food whenever he goes to a buffet. He's lost a lot of weight. He also desires longevity. He thinks he'd like to visit the Hunzas who live in Tibet. Anyway, Hunzas have a tradition of only working for half a day and playing the rest of the day. They play all sorts of games. Of course, they live in pure air and eat a lot of fruits and vegetables.

Kevin's goal is to live to be 110. He is cultivating relaxation. The two of them are now going to flotation tanks once a week and getting massages and giving massages. He tells me she looks radiant. He certainly looks better than I've ever seen him."

"It all sounds great to me. I wish I had met him." I interrupt Samson again.

"Well, I believe in the human potential movement and I subscribe to a lot of what Kevin and Kiki are doing. But I've got this feeling that it's not going to work out. Kevin is a charismatic Catholic. He is not divorced. Kiki is <u>not</u>, according to Kevin, the mistress type. She's a fine lady.

I just have this feeling there's going to be trouble. Kevin's wife has been around for a long time. They have children and grandchildren. Who knows? I'm just skeptical."

"I have to know what's going to happen," I said.""May I call you in several months, in October, let's say, to get updated?"

"Sure, but time is up now. It was fun talking to you."

End of Part I of Samson's Tale

I continued my research, but I kept thinking of Samson's friend Kevin. What a story! I had no idea that people could become so passionate in their sixties. I had no idea that misery could make way for such bliss. I couldn't wait to talk to Samson again and find out what had happened. Meanwhile I practiced yoga and got massages. I didn't go to flotation tanks, but I did cut out meat from my diet and I began to eat more fruit and veggies. I tried to meditate, but I kept falling asleep almost immediately. Soon, several months had passed. It was October.

PART II OF SAMSON'S TALE

I called Samson and he brought me up to date. Kevin had moved out of his house and taken his clothes to Kiki's house. They bought a tent and went camping on weekends. Kiki had never camped before. Kevin made up stories about the people who emerged from their tents with hair curlers and kitchen chairs and grills, more equipment than you could imagine. He would make up dialogues between the couples who sat silently. . Kiki laughed till her ribs hurt. Kevin invented stories about their past lives together, how they had met as two shepherds in Yugoslavia several centuries ago, how they had lived in Iceland and had been lovers.

They went swimming in the ocean. Kevin loved to enclose her in his arms and swim with her on his belly. They synchronized strokes. They played like dolphins. Water was their favorite element. On land they played in bed. Their happiness together was unbounded.

Then, Kevin's wife heard he was seeing another woman. She came back from New York and confronted him. She pleaded with him to return to her. She had always loved him, she said, and had been a good mother and grandmother. She had always been faithful to him, never even entertained the thought of another man. This argument carried a lot of weight with him.

Finally when Kevin told his wife he couldn't give up Kiki and live the way he used to, she began to compromise. She knew that he loved going to the symphony on Tuesdays. She knew he had waited years to get good orchestra seats. They had shared that waiting and the pleasure of being there. She asked if he would continue to take her there on Tuesdays and take her out on Saturday nights. That was all she would ask for, other than financial support. Kevin went home to Kiki and proposed this arrangement.

Kiki was furious with him for the first time. He became glum. Kevin decided, because of the tension, they should go away for a week to the Yucatan. Kevin needed to get some perspective. Immediately, Kevin's wife had an automobile accident. She could have been killed, but she suffered only broken cartilage. She threw out the possibility that she would commit suicide. Kevin became more alarmed. Kicki tried to suggest that Kevin's wife was being manipulative.

In spite of all this, Kiki and Kevin went to the Yucatan and had an ecstatic time. They stayed in a Club Med in the jungle. Bougainvillea cascaded into the pool outside their door. They were alone and desperately in love. Kevin told me he hardly slept. He guarded her all night. He didn't want to close his eyes, to miss one moment of being with her. But when they came back to Philadelphia, Kevin suddenly shouted in the airport, "There's my wife."

He actually saw a woman who looked like his wife, coming toward him, coming to reclaim him. Kiki grew alarmed. She thought he might be going mad. He was hallucinating. So when they went back to her house, she asked if he would play the pendulum game they had played many times together.

"What is the pendulum game?" I asked.

Samson explained, "You have to hang a ring or some heavy object on a string. You then choose directions by asking the pendulum, 'Which direction is *yes?*' The pendulum moves in a direction, north and south, for example. Then you ask the pendulum to choose *no.* It will move, for example, east and west. Then you can ask for other directions: diagonal for *maybe,* around and around for *I don't want to talk about that."*

Kevin asked for the direction of yes: it registered north and south. Then he asked for no: east and west. He stopped asking. Kiki began questioning him. He concentrated.

"Does Kevin love Kiki? The pendulum swung madly north and south.

"Is Kevin going to marry Kiki?" The pendulum reluctantly swung slowly east and west.

"Is it because he can't get divorced?" The pendulum shamefacedly, hesitatingly swung north and south.

Kiki and Kevin looked at each other. She knew she was getting honest answers from Kevin's mind. She began to cry. Kevin held her and kissed her over and over again. Kiki was not the mistress type. She wanted him completely: body, mind and soul. Their connection was so deep that she knew she would have to give him up. She did not want to destroy his sanity with such a conflict. He knew what she knew and they both agreed they had to stop seeing each other. She begged him to wean her slowly. She knew it would be too cruel to stop abruptly. They had spoken to each other on the phone almost all day long when they were apart. His heart hurt when he wasn't with her. Kevin had told me this repeatedly.

She begged him. She wanted him to see her several times a week and then only twice a week, and then only once a week and then once every two weeks and then only once a month. But he felt he couldn't do that. It had to be cold turkey. He needed all or nothing, quickly, slicing her out of his heart.

He knew his decision was influenced by his Catholicism. He was also afraid his wife would kill herself. And then there was the conventional, ethical judge in him that said he was doing something illegal and wrong. He was a grandfather and a father and a husband. But mostly, I think, there was cowardice."

"Wasn't Kiki being inflexible? If she loved him so much," I questioned, "why didn't she compromise her position?"

Samson concluded. "Maybe they were doomed to suffer. Kevin is seeing a heart specialist. He has lost his buoyancy. He says it feels as though his chest has caved in. He had me touch his chest to show me a cavity that was never there before. Only time will tell if he's going to have a heart attack. It makes me terribly sad to see him this way."

"But think of all the joy they've had together," I insisted. "They truly found happiness. I would love to meet such a man, even if the love affair had to end. I'm not a romantic, but this story wakes up irrational urges in me. Look how alive they became. Look at all the memories they have. That's almost immortality. She'll be able to grow old and remember the moments they had of bliss, of pure, unadulterated delight. I bet most women would give up a lot for such an adventure."

I listened to myself raving. I thought I was not a romantic. But this wonderful tale had moved me deeply. When I returned to a more critical state, I vowed never to get involved with a man who was separated, but not divorced, particularly a man who was Catholic.

Are you looking for a grand passion? Could you fall for a man who would bring you to life sexually, but might not be free to marry?

VI

"The worst fear is the fear of living."

– Teddy Roosevelt

John: the entrepreneur

John had so many degrees it was difficult to get them all on the "Best and Brightest" profile page. He had the usual MIT, Harvard degrees. But, he also had an MBA, a JD, a BEE, and a CPA and a diplome from the Sorbonne. He listed his profession as an investor. He was divorced, had three children and was "handsome, athletic, slender and well-dressed." He was also fluent in French.

His list of hobbies included: the fine arts, the opera, classical music, downhill skiing, hiking, sea kayaking, antiquing, collecting studio glass and textiles, movie going, language study, reading and charitable work with teenagers.

The last hobby stood out. John was the only person whose profile mentioned charitable work. He told me he had started a foundation for teenage boys in trouble. His own father had died when he was four. His mother was still alive and, from what he told me, he loved her without ambivalence. This statement, I felt, was particularly significant. I am always more trusting of men who truly loved their mothers.

John was also very proud of his father who had served bravely in World War II and of the three children he had fathered while married to his one and only wife. He admitted that when he was pursuing his careers in real estate, accounting, law and consulting work, his wife had to care for the children all the time. He respected mothers and motherhood.

"Children take the rough edges off of us," he sighed. "I can tell when I meet a woman whether she's had kids or not."

He described himself as a positive thinker, and under the question regarding "what you think you have to offer," he listed responsibility, commitment, flexibility, generosity, good health and an interesting life style. He sounded wonderful to me, someone who enjoys his life, someone with high energy who is aware of his spiritual, intellectual and physical attributes. That is a rare combination.

It was summer when I spoke to him. He had extensive plans.

"I'm climbing Mt.******," he said, "and then I'm going to St. Petersburg to see the Hermitage. After that I'm going sea kayaking in Alaska." I heard him say. "I'll be back in September."

I was struck by the diversity of his interests, the vigorous nature of his activities, the sheer miles he would cover in a few months.

"I'm amazed you're still single. Why did you get divorced? How have you remained single for seven years?"

"Let's just say my wife and I grew in opposite directions. She remained in a small town of 5,000 people and I went to Paris to study French for a year."

"But you're so exciting, so alive," I said. I could feel I had lost all objectivity.

"I'm looking for a best friend and someone with the right chemistry. She can be independent, but she has to have a sense of humor. She has to be romantic and practical. She has to be my equal financially. I don't want a woman who feels inferior to me. She has to have a fine character. I'm not an ideologue, but I'm conservative economically. I'm passionate and compassionate. I want that in her too. She has to be considerate and monogamous. These traits are difficult to find in combination."

At that point it was midnight and he started interviewing me. By two A.M. we were both groggy.

"How about sending me your profile and a picture. I'll get in touch with you in September when I come back," he murmured

Then reality hit me. I couldn't climb mountains. I'd never been in a kayak in my life. I was five years older than this man. I probably was penniless in comparison to him.

" I don't think I could keep up with you physically," I said.

He said, "I wasn't thinking about that. I was thinking you'd be a great person to go to the Hermitage with. I'd like to take you to concerts and museums and plays. I'd like to celebrate Bastille Day with you in Paris."

"Yes, yes, I'd love that. I'll send you a package of stuff. Anything. Everything."

My steaming brain had turned off.

"But who will you go kayaking with?" I asked one last question." Aren't there beautiful women who go on those trips"?

"Yes, there are," he replied.""In fact, I had to share my tent with one the last time I went."

My heart sank.

"She turned out to be a lesbian," he laughed.

In September he didn't call. When I finally called him in October, he explained his mother had been hospitalized. He was so busy taking care of her and finding an adequate nursing home, he couldn't think about anything else. He said he would call.

I never heard from him. I speculated, of course, on why this happened. Since I had spoken to him in July and it was now October, I wondered if he had found someone else. He even returned my letters and the material I had sent him, but not my poem. Oh well, these things happen. Nothing ventured, nothing gained. Most people do not want to explain themselves or give excuses for lack of interest. Besides, I had probably saved my knees, I thought, remembering a mountain climber I had dated. I was stupid enough to go to mountain climbing school to keep up with him.

My knees have never been the same; I remembered all this, while munching on sour grapes.

> Would you be able to keep up with John? Are you looking for someone who is a mountain climber, tennis partner, hiker and adventurer?

VII

*"Will you consent to be
my many-branched, small and dearest tree?"*

– Delmore Schwartz

Drake, a professional story teller, and his wife, Juliet, who fell in love with a man named Romeo.

When I was visiting friends in Denver, Colorado, I met someone who was a professional storyteller. He and I were the same age. His hair was turning gray and he had an engaging leprechaun personality. He was short, trim, energetic and friendly. He was, of course, Irish. He told me his father had invented the process of candling eggs for inspection. He said his mother had been harsh and domineering. Drake was an only child. His father suffered from depressions and Drake's job was to cheer him up by telling him stories.

As an adult, Drake had worked as an administrator for a community-based organization that helped troubled teenagers. Drake had married a woman whom he described as "strange," but he said he had loved her dearly. She had a mother who lived with them and who fought with him continually about the kitchen floor. She thought that she should be washing and waxing it and Drake insisted upon doing that chore alone. The minute Drake washed the floor, the mother-in-law tramped all over it, leaving her footprints. One day, he put a heavy chair in front of the door and waited. The mother-in-law knocked over the chair and walked across the floor, muttering, "God damn executive."

Nevertheless, he was fond of the old biddy and still visited her occasionally.

Drake's wife turned out to be schizophrenic, needing many hospitalizations. Drake finally divorced her. He married almost immediately, a beautiful, sexy, aerobics teacher. He was blissfully happy until he found out that she was having an affair with a man named Romeo. This Romeo, it seems, worked overtime. His moonlighting job was delivering corpses to the morgue. Drake's wife was meeting Romeo at the morgue, after the delivery. They had a special room where they would rendezvous.

Drake was, of course, furious and when he found out that Romeo was married, he went to Romeo's house to see Romeo's wife, a heavy, Italian woman named Rosa. She was wearing one of those muumuus that look like a tent filled with helium, like a Nikkei de St. Phaal sculpture. Rosa offered him rum cake and fruit. Drake refused the food and went right for the jugular.

"Look, Mrs. Ficcocelli, I'm here to discuss a very nasty situation between my wife and your husband. "

"Mr. Drake, what's my Romeo gotta do wid your wife?"

"I hate to tell you this. Haven't you suspected that something is wrong? Isn't Romeo coming home late on certain nights?"

"Yeah, Romeo has two jobs. He delivas bodies to da morgue on Tuesdays and Thursdays. He likes to play poker wid some a his friends on Wednesday. Romeo is a good man. He gives me money and likes me to live well. I leave him lasagna and meat loaf, so he'll have a good meal when he gets home."

"I hate to tell you this. I really do. But to be blunt, your Romeo is fucking my Juliet in the morgue on Tuesdays and Thursdays."

"Awwwh, get out a here. What do ya think I am, a dummy? I'm gonna believe you, a stranger? My Romeo is a good man. He brings home da bacon. Whoever your wife is doin it wit, it ain't my Romeo."

Needless to say, Drake had a difficult time convincing Rosa to divorce Romeo so that Romeo would marry Drake's wife.

One night Drake hid in the morgue and took photos of the assignation. He showed the photos to Rosa. That did it. Rosa finally told Romeo she wanted a divorce. Romeo then married Juliet after Drake divorced her and all should have been well.

A year later, Drake met his ex-wife looking terrible, thin and nervous. She asked if she could wash and dry her clothes at Drake's house.

" But Juliet, why do you want to do that?"

Drake found out from Juliet that Romeo was in a "menage a trois" and she was doing the laundry and cooking and cleaning for two men who were part of the triangle. She was miserable. She had never guessed that Romeo was bisexual.

I thought that Drake was putting me on. After all, his story was getting a bit kinky, and it was coming from a man who told stories for a living. But I decided to believe him. He didn't seem to experience malice toward his first wife, his mother-in-law or his second marriage partner, Juliet.

I asked Drake if he was in a relationship at the moment. I asked what type of woman he was now looking for.

He replied," You know, Minerva, I'm a bit discouraged. The women I've met lately are just too aggressive sexually for my taste. The other day I was invited to a party and the woman who threw the party asked me to stay later and tried to seduce me. I thought she was a perfectly proper lady. When I refused to undress, she called me an odd duck. She thought that was what men wanted."

"I'm not a Romeo. I don't need that kind of pressure. I enjoy women who are kind and sweet and tiny and neat, who wait for me to make the first move, which I never do unless I know the person well and feel comfortable with her."

Drake confessed he had been in a sort of relationship with a dancing partner for several years. She was hounding him and he had lost interest in her, except as a dancing partner.

"I want to get out of her clutches. She's constantly calling me and I don't want to take her out to dinner or go to bed with her."

I told Drake I was hearing the voice of a man who felt like a victim. Once more he had gotten involved with the wrong woman. The situation was more taxing than rewarding. I reminded him of what he had told me about his father and depression. He recalled that his father was fired during one of his depressions. He had already told me he had spent a lot of time with his father, trying to help him.

"Drake, is it possible that you are reconstructing the same kind of situation in your adult relationships? You seem to be finding women who are a source of pain, rather than pleasure. Perhaps you associate intimacy with sharing pain? Are you trying to repeat your relationship with your father, rather than your mother? I'm not a psychologist, but somehow it doesn't make sense that a funny, attractive man like you can't find a satisfying partner."

He thought about my speculations and then answered," Yes, I think you are right, Minerva. I didn't realize I was looking for my father, not my mother. Thanks for your help. Thanks. Let me pay for dinner."

Since I had given him the benefit of my $20,000 worth of analysis, I decided to accept his offer.

What is your tolerance level for neurotic men? Do you enjoy meeting men who are "different?" Drake has a sense of humor and he is a sweet guy. Would you date him?

VIII

"The refusal of ecstasy is unknown in heaven."

– Marianne Williamson

Hollis, the architect, in love with Beatrice

While on vacation in San Miguel de Allende, four hours north of Mexico City, I met a widower from Canada. He was tall, thin, handsome, witty, debonair, a bit of a dandy when he wore his white Panama and a stunning, white, summer suit. He looked like an older Dick Diver out of *Tender Is the Night*. He was a patrician whose appearance equaled the appearance of the woman beside him. She was elegant and obviously refined. We met at dinner at our pension, El Mansion Del Bosque.

When Beatrice, the elegant beauty with white hair and blue eyes, heard about my book, she said, "Oh, do Hollis, please, Minerva. We're not married. He's still single and over sixty. I'd love to know what he says he wants—even if I have to read it in a book."

That very night I interviewed Hollis and we started with his happy Canadian childhood. Hollis grew up in a small town on Lake Ontario. His father commuted to Toronto to work as an architect. It was during the Great Depression and they were poor. But his mother always said,

"We may be poor, but you always have the best shoes. You'll always have the best shoes."

Hollis' father was opposed to private schools and fraternities; so Hollis went to regular, public schools and was popular enough to run for president of his high school. He met his "wife-to-be" as a farmerette.

"In those days we were an item," he chuckled. It was 1946 when teenagers went off to farms in the summer to pick strawberries or something. Hollis and his sweetheart couldn't marry for five years, since Hollis had to complete his university degree. Naturally she stayed a virgin till the wedding day. That's the way it was then. They did travel with friends in Europe, but were always careful to uphold appearances. Hollis slept in a room with his male friends and Eleanor slept in a room with the other girls.

"I remember vividly the day before the wedding when my aunt came to visit and my mother said, 'Oh, Hollis is outside in the garden, preparing his torso in the sun.' Eleanor was busy doing everything that needed to be done before the wedding. Her mother was dead and she had to be the organizer of it all. She was always quiet and competent, trim and tiny, only five feet two inches."

Later, Hollis told me, they had two boys in 1956 and 1958. One is a stand-up comic. The other is in business.

"Both are splendid chaps," Hollis boasted.""Our second son also plays the guitar professionally. They are six feet two and six feet four. Neither is prepared to marry yet. They love each other as few brothers do. They both adored their mother. Eleanor's illness and death have been hard on them, perhaps harder than for me, since I took care of her and finally watched her die."

Eleanor had open-heart surgery. She recovered, but then developed other ailments. Suddenly, ten years later, her torn heart collapsed.

"I was devastated," moaned Hollis. "But because she had been ill, I had time to grieve before she died. I was very fortunate. Women started asking me to dinner almost immediately after the funeral. Beatrice, the woman I'm in love with, invited me along with some other friends. She had lost her husband several years before Eleanor left me. We had been social friends for years. In fact, I was her architect. I knew her husband well. When you design a home you get to know people profoundly. If you want to know what I want, Beatrice is the person I want."

"Is she like your wife?" I asked. I explained that many widowers are looking for the same kind of woman who made them happy.

"She's not at all similar to my wife," Hollis answered. "Beatrice can be quite bossy. My wife was quieter and more reserved, less opinionated. But Beatrice has a fine character and a great sense of humor. She's quick. She's also very loving to my sons. Frankly, she's also quite smashing, don't you think?"

"Yes, I do. She's striking. Quite beautiful."

"There's really only one thing that bothers me. She has this thing about her space. She jokes about wanting two condos next to each other. For me, physical closeness is very important. I suppose I'd like us to live in the same house, but I think it's going to take time. For now, I know we're doing the right things, enjoying each other, not worrying too much about what people think."

"I'd like to look after her more, of course. I suppose the word "independent" sums it up. Her need to be independent! She, for example, insists that we split costs when we travel together. We're both well off, so that's fine if it's what she wants. Probably the biggest difference between Beatrice and my wife is that Beatrice criticizes me. I think it's funny. But I often do what she tells me to do. That's what I mean by "bossiness.""

"So, if you could have whatever you wanted, what would it be?" I asked.

"I'd say it would be that she and I live in the same house, not necessarily married, but married in spirit, not so she would cook or take care of me. I'm a better cook than she is. I guess it's just her presence that I want—the fact that she is there, somewhere in the house—just there."

The next day, I sat next to Beatrice at lunch and chatted quietly with her about my interview with Hollis. I told her he was an excellent addition to my book because he had been and still is a happy man. Yes, he had lost his wife, but apparently he had a good marriage. He had grieved enough. He was not depressed or morbidly connected to her.

"Well, he's probably told you that I won't live with him, but that in time I will change my attitude. What he won't accept is that I love him, but I'm not in love with him. I don't want to be with him **all the time.**"

"Poor Hollis," I answered. "He's so clearly in love with you. Yes, I see he wants your presence. It's really going to make him suffer not to have you in the same house with him."

Postscript to Hollis and Beatrice

At first I thought: What will happen to this couple? She loves him, but isn't in love. He loves her, but can't accept her wish to be separate. Oh my. It's an Indecision Rag. Isn't it a shame they can't love each other to the same degree and in the same way?

What I've seen from my vantage point of seventy years is that there are many ways in which couples can relate. Remember the tales about knights and chastity belts. Remember the sixties and the trials of open marriages.

I happen to know people who are happily married who have lived together for forty years. The husband has a lover whom he sees on Thursdays. The wife has one she sees the same day. They both have come to accept this arrangement. It is an unusual one, perhaps, in the United States. But it is possible for the people I know. Does that shock you?

I also know couples who spend a great deal of time separated. Either because of his work or, in rarer cases, her work, they are only together for half of the year. They love each other and they love their children. They keep in touch through Email and telephone calls. And when they are back together, it's like a holiday. Maybe it isn't an ideal arrangement, but this couple makes it work.

There are couples who sustain a relationship for years and years, even though the adventurous husband has periodic affairs when he is traveling. This is more common than the adventurous woman traveling. But a book about women's erotic life, *The Erotic Silence of the American Wife* by Dalma Heyn indicates that women have the same fantasies that men do about needing more than one erotic attachment. I know I couldn't accept these deviations, but obviously there are others who can. Look at Hilary Clinton, for example.

What intrigued me about Hollis and Beatrice was that this marvelous couple who looked as wedded and respectable as any couple I could imagine, were not wedded and didn't care whether they were or not. I have since met many couples like them, traveling together, partnered, but not yoked by law.

> How has this phenomenon come about? And is it going to expand? The only statistic I have is from that November, 2003 AARP study which states that households headed by a person over 45 or older containing two adults not married to each other have increased dramatically since 1995. The figure was 1.2 million households.

I will raise these questions again in my conclusion and discuss a number of solutions to the longevity issue and the desires for separation and freedom along with attachment, intimacy and friendship.

But let's get back to my stories. At the same pension where I met Hollis, there was a man and his fiancée. His name was Joe. Her name was Margaret. They were from California and she was a honeysuckle blonde. Joe had heard of my interview with Hollis and the next night he told me he was over sixty and technically still single. His wife-to-be thought it would help my book to add him to my group of good men. She was sure his story would interest me. So I agreed to interview him after dinner. We walked next door to the Jacaranda Hotel. He also liked hot fudge sundaes. That was the price I was paying for several hours of questions and responses.

IX

"All that rescues us is love."

– Heinrich Heine

Joe, a corporate executive who believes in angels.

Joe was six feet tall, handsome, a bit stocky and in love with what I had thought all men wanted, especially Jewish men. Margaret was a Christian angel.

Of course, the Jews had invented angels: the seraphim and the cherubim, the archangels and the great fallen angel named Satan. But the Christians made them beautiful and blonde and blue-eyed like Margaret.

Joe told me he had grown up in Brooklyn, New York in an immigrant Jewish family. He had ended up in Florida majoring in marketing at the University of Florida. As an adolescent he played a lot of sports. His career was predictably meteoric. In his thirties he floated up to the top of the corporation he worked for. The senior guys liked him. He said he had been a bit of a visionary, using his imagination to create new products

Along the way he married an airline stewardess. They had two children, a boy and a girl. It was his view of a traditional marriage. He brought home the bacon, lots of it, and she was supposed to be the homebody and take care of the children. They stayed married for thirty-seven years.

But in her mid-life, she awakened to find she had no identity. Since she had been much younger than Joe when she married, she had not lived out her youth. At fifty-nine she was confused and excessively dependent on him. Psychologists convinced her she should separate. They had diagnosed her as manic-depressive. She was on medication. Joe described her as manipulative, secretive and deceptive.

Her mania manifested itself in periodic purchases of hotels. She said she wanted to own the Fairmont in San Francisco. Of course she had no experience running hotels and, consequently, her purchases ended in debacles. During the three years they were separated, Joe entered therapy with her. They sold their house and he gave her plenty of money to decorate a new, splendid castle. He conceded that he spent too much time on his own entrepreneurial merry-go-round and that he would cut back. He promised to take her on more vacations and trips with him.

While he was doing his best in good faith to understand himself and her better, she was secretly seeing a guy whom she had known in high school. Joe's philosophy was that marriage was forever, in spite of a few affairs. Obviously those affairs were supposed to be his, not hers. He felt betrayed at the highest level when he found out about her clandestine adventures. Twelve days before Christmas, she left him a "gutless" note saying that she was filing for a divorce.

The divorce was not yet final. He had waged a war with himself about valuations of property. It was in his best interests to speed things up. But she wanted to delay the divorce. It had been in process for three years.

He had been dating many types of women. When he met Margaret, he knew she was the one.

"She knows who she is. Not like my wife who has been unsure of herself for years and years," Joe emphasized.

"She also knows who I am, a man who needs to rule the house. I've been successful in the system. I don't have to come home to feel hen-pecked. I want to be happy, healthy and wise. When you're younger, you like to jump into empty pools without water. You take risks. You get hurt. You gamble. But when you're my age, you want to be with a woman who is truly loving. Margaret has a Scandinavian personality. She knows what's important. She doesn't laugh at me when I say I believe in angels. In fact, she believes in them too. Tomorrow is her birthday and I'm going to show you what I got for her."

He pulled out of his pocket a gift, wrapped in a silk envelope: a gorgeous, golden angel. I gasped at its beauty and its symbolic meaning. I knew she would love it. This man had found what he wanted, a woman who was the opposite of his first wife.

X

*"Marriage, if one will face the truth,
is an evil, but a necessary evil."*

– Menander

Vincent, an architect with a vision

My stay in San Miguel was fruitful. In my yoga class, I met a charming man, an African American, also six feet tall, handsome, dressed like Richard Gregory wearing a crocheted hat made of multi-colored threads.

Vincent informed me that he had grown up in California. His grandfather's second wife was a founder of a black college and his grandfather was the son of an overseer of a plantation.

Vincent was light skinned, from a racially mixed heritage. He said the best thing he had done was to leave home at fifteen to live with an uncle who was a writer. Vincent was flunking out of high school when he moved into his uncle's house. But within a year he was on the honor roll.

"That's the difference between a kid with an alcoholic father and a kid living with a disciplined, caring, intelligent adult," Vincent concluded.

Vincent eventually became an architect and city planner. In fact, I was surprised to find out that he had designed the center of the neighborhood I had lived in for several months. His theme was unifying different ethnic neighborhoods by creating spaces that stimulate gathering and chatting, places where human beings could relax and be part of a community. It was what he loved most about San Miguel de Allende, its human scale, and its disdain for malls or suburban transportation.

San Miguel was like the neighborhood Vincent had designed: connected, charmingly informal, walkable, and full of volunteerism and a spirit of caring.

Vincent had worked for international firms and decided to start his own architectural firm. In addition, he was a political activist, having served as president of a chapter of the NAACP. However, two tragic threads ran through his life: his father's alcoholism which led to suicide and inappropriate women. Vincent's first wife was a young, Jewish radical. They had two children. According to Vincent she was a wet blanket, always dampening him down.

41

" I would say she was a woman of small ambition. We got together because of our political interests and because of the sexual revolution."

His second wife had an alcohol problem, which was the cause of her early death. She was beautiful but sexually repressed, an ex-nun of German and Irish heritage. "We had a wild time together," Vincent remarked nostalgically.

"But she drank just like my father. After her death, I went to Santa Fe. I gave up on civil rights. Nixon and Reagan weren't doing a damn thing for blacks. I decided to market Native American products: a different way of helping an oppressed group. That was where I met my latest nemesis, the baroness, from whom I'm currently getting divorced. I had open-heart surgery when I was with my second wife, a ten-year marriage. The baroness picked me up in Santa Fe and is dropping me in San Miguel," he confessed without apparent anger.

Again, Vincent repeated that he had some good times with her, but this time he had fewer kind words.

"She was the kind of woman who eats you up and when she's had enough, leaves you on an island in Indonesia with congestive heart failure. That's exactly what she did to me. Imagine, just imagine, what it's like to be in a hospital in Jakarta, that pollution-ridden hellhole. They sent me there by helicopter from Sulawesi. I don't understand why I'm still alive.

Anyway, what we've done together was to build a huge estate here in San Miguel. When I discovered this city, I knew it was where I wanted to spend the rest of my days. Cities in the US are getting worse and worse, losing all human qualities. Here you can hang out, just as you and I are hanging out, talking and having lunch at the Pegaso. It doesn't matter here how much money you make. All that matters is how you are with other people. I poured my heart into building this mansion. I'll be damned if I let her have it. I'm in the middle of trying to buy her out. What I want to do is turn the place into a great meditation center. I'll bring wonderful thinkers and spiritual people, who will open up people who want to live without shopping malls, who want to promenade in the village square, sit in small cafes and restaurants and know all the shopkeepers and enjoy the light in San Miguel.

As for what I want now, with my ticker and my experience of mortality, I never want to marry again. But, that doesn't mean I have to be alone. There are many interesting, single women here."

As we ended our lunch, several of the waiters had been standing nearby to pay their respects to Vincent. Everyone seemed to know him. Everyone nodded and smiled his way during our meal. The owner of the Pegaso came to the table and shook hands with him. He then insisted that we have a drink on the house.

I could see that Vincent's dream was a reality. This town was the community he wanted to live in, a place where he felt at home, respected and appreciated by the locals, a place where kindness flowed out to people who liked you, liked your beingness, " not just your pocket book or your powerful status."

Are you looking for an idealistic man? Would you want to have Vincent as a friend? Remember where I met him. In my yoga class. If you follow your interests, you can meet men who are interesting everywhere.

XI

"The soul that beholds beauty becomes beautiful."

– PBS film on Buddhism with Huston Smith

Murray, a psychologist, professor of oriental medicine, a writer and a complete human being

After my visit to San Miguel de Allende, I spent some time in San Francisco where friends told me I <u>had</u> to meet Murray. "Murray is unique," they said. "He would make a great addition to your book about single men. He's 79, a young 79. He still is parachuting out of airplanes. He's been doing it long before ex-President Bush thought about it. He is ageless."

These friends gave me Murray's phone number and we decided we would all meet for dinner. Afterwards, I would interview Murray privately. When Murray entered the restaurant, I saw that his physical appearance was striking. He had a large frame, a high forehead, large eagle beak, and majestic torso. He looked amazingly alert. His eyes were penetrating my core. He was the epitome of virility. But his voice was soft and deep. He talked like a man who was used to being listened to, a man who was paid to listen.

During dinner I also learned that Murray was both the family psychotherapist of my friends and their all purpose guru. I was impressed with his wide range of interests, accomplishments and experience. I learned that he came from Detroit to Hollywood in the forties and wrote screen plays as well as plays for the theater. He had been a "card carrying Commie," and very vulnerable to the waves of McCarthyism that swept out many prolific and distinguished writers in the early fifties.

Leaving Hollywood, he stepped into clinical psychology, perhaps because he found it difficult to understand the phenomenon that McCarthy represented. He spent years in clinical practice until a day when he was asked to be co-director of a panel with professional psychologists who claimed they had mystical experiences. The other presenter was a philosopher from Stanford who was pro ESP. Murray was chosen because of his skepticism. He had never had such experiences. He would fill the role of neutrality that the panel required.

However, after the conference, in spite of the fact that he consciously believed he had been in the presence of psychotics on that panel, he dreamed that one of his patients called him up and asked him to write a recommendation for her. She was going to London to a job interview and felt that his support would be invaluable. The next day, lo and behold, that same patient was in his office and the conversation he had experienced in his dream was repeated verbatim. This incident and others like it peaked his curiosity and interest in ESP, intuitive leaps and other psychic occurrences. Murray got involved with LSD, but had to take it 200 times before it had any effect on him. "That shows you how skeptical I was, " he told me.

Murray then became involved with a research group which turned Aldous Huxley on to LSD. Huxley later wrote an influential book about psychic breakthroughs called *The Doors of Perception and the Gates of Hell*. Murray also began teaching workshops involving the power of the mind to control behavior.

This was a period of unusual growth for Murray. Just like the "Silva Mind Control" workshops, Murray's workshops became famous and he traveled all over the world. His interest in alternative medicine broadened and slowly he acquired a degree that would allow him to practice and teach oriental medicine. He became a professor at a college of oriental medicine where he told his students it was not obligatory to come to class. Everyone would get an A,— regardless of participation. What they **had** to do was to produce a paper that was interesting, original and perhaps publishable. The students flocked to his lectures and he became the most popular faculty member at the college.

Recently, however, Murray had a wake-up call in the form of a heart attack. He had undergone a triple bypass operation. Knowing that every day could be his last, he decided to accept his death each night before he goes to sleep. "I die daily," he said.

Murray is not a stranger to death, since two of his four wives have died. The first and last wives were women he deeply loved. One could still feel his passion and devotion to each of them whenever he spoke of these two women. The first wife had died of Hodgkin's disease. She and Murray lived together for twenty-one years, sixteen of which she had been ill. They had a son whom Murray loved very much and now a daughter-in-law and a grandson whom he was crazy about.

The fourth wife was also a profoundly passionate liaison, a woman like his first wife who was a painter. He could talk with her for hours on end. At our second meeting (because Murray and I found that several hours at my apartment were not enough time to cover his whole story), I saw the paintings by his second wife. They were haunting, abstract landscapes, often divided into triptychs, incredible both in their color and in the emptiness that comes only when thoughts stop. They were the landscapes of a seeing eyeball, detached and mysterious.

Fate had given Murray another opportunity to care for a woman who made him perfectly happy. This fourth wife developed Alzheimer's ten years before she died. Murray told me a story that made me weep. He said that Marlon Brando was a patient of his. Murray was still practicing medicine. One day Brando called and Murray's wife answered the phone.

"Is Murray there?" Brando asked.

"Yes, he is," she answered and then hung up the phone.

Brando called back. Again she answered and said, "Yes, he is." She again hung up the phone.

After several more repetitions, Murray heard the phone and answered it himself.

"Boy, you have a problem," Brando commented.

"Tell me about it", replied Murray sardonically.

"Have you gotten any help to take care of her?" Brando asked

"You know I'm not bourgeois enough to have saved any money," Murray answered.

Then Murray told me Brando insisted on giving Murray $2000 a month until Murray had his wife admitted to a nursing home. Needless to say, this was generosity that Murray would never forget.

You're probably wondering, as I was, whatever happened to the other two wives? He married the second wife for two and one half years.

" I didn't know her well," Murray explained.

"Why did you get divorced?" I pursued.

"Well, she turned out to be acutely neurotic. She tried to kill herself twice and then she tried to kill me. I concluded she didn't like me."

This was Murray's way of saying he's not infallible.

"I can have my head up my ass just like anyone else," was his answer.

The third wife turned out to be another mistake. She was manic-depressive.

"Those were days when I was too attached to my feelings. I was lonely. She was a depressive type who brought everyone down. We've been good friends since the separation and divorce, however. Now when I am unhappy, I'm not unhappy about being unhappy. I've grown in the sense that I don't feel important anymore. Occasionally, if I'm taken by surprise or abused, my old anger flares up, but generally I let things pass...like clouds in a swift wind."

As we continued to talk, a fly started buzzing around the room. Murray opened the window wider and then the door.

"We have to give this creature the chance to go back to its space."

I asked Murray, "Do you refrain from killing all insects?"

"Before LSD, I didn't feel any affinity to flies. After LSD, I know we're connected."

" Murray, you are unique. What's more, you're the most lovable man I've interviewed. Tell me, what do you want now, this instant, at seventy-nine?" I asked with complete admiration.

"I would say that I have what I want. There are three women in my life. One is a labor union organizer; the second is an erotic attachment, a woman who's married to a Bill Gates type who flies down to meet me every few weeks. The third is a performance artist who makes me laugh. When we make love, the Goddess of Sex descends. She and I really experience self-transcendence."

"I don't want to be presumptuous or intrusive but it sounds to me as though you've divided your desires into three women who represent mind, body and spirit separately. With your first and last wives, you were able to find all in one person. Now it's more like a union organizer for the mind, an erotic lady for the body and a performance artist for your spirit."

"You may be right, Minerva. But overall, I think you should conclude that I've had wonderful women in my life. They are all my closest friends and my fellow explorers. The mistake most men make is that they are too goal oriented. What matters most is establishing a deep friendship. That is finally what lasts the longest. I do believe it is the most precious of all rewards."

"Murray, I couldn't agree with you more. Friends have provided both continuity and change for me. They have become my family. Usually they reflect back images of me at my best. They remind me in dark times of the joys I've experienced. They're the ones I count on to be there for me, and I, for them, till death us does part. I feel married to my friends. I hope you'll be one of them, Murray. I'm really honored to know you."

"Listen, Minerva, I've enjoyed these interviews as much as you have. I want you to use my real name. I've given up worrying about how I'm seen. I'd like your readers to know me and see me as I am."

"That's great, Murray. You know what I was thinking? I've just interviewed another man from California and I'm somewhat troubled as to how I should present him. I have mixed feelings about him. I guess I'd like to send you the copy and see what you think."

"I'll do that gladly. I think what you're doing is describing character types. I'd like to see a few of them. And I'll give you my reactions for whatever it's worth."

So, I sent Murray the following profile of Walter Wingo:

XII

"There is no man so good, who, were he to submit all his thoughts and actions to the laws, would not deserve hanging ten times in his life."

– Montaigne

Walter Wingo, the Watsu Practitioner

When I was visiting friends in Palo Alto, I met a man who was a perpetual seeker, a watsu practitioner. For those of you who don't know anything about watsu, think of it as a relaxing massage in very warm water, water that you can float in. In that water, there is a transference of energy, through the practitioner to you. Picture yourself being held gently in warm water and swished about, allowing yourself to let go, release all tension and allow your body to receive the manipulation of muscles in troubled areas of your body where there are muscle knots or even scars from past injuries. All of this is supposed to lead to a mystical experience of cosmic proportions, a transcendent lifting into a higher state of consciousness or a feeling of oneness with the universe.

I had been suffering from a blocked scapula for years and my massage therapist in Hartford could never figure out how to unlock it. Whenever I visited friends in California, I would hear about the latest way to massage therapeutically to reach troublesome areas. When I heard about watsu, I quickly found a local practitioner.

This individual, we'll call him Walter, was born in New Jersey. He was sixty-one years old and he grew up mostly in the company of women— his mother and his grandmother. He blamed his father's early departure on his grandmother who deliberately broke up her daughter's marriage. Because they lived over a funeral home, Walter remembers having to be quiet a lot when there was a funeral going on.

After I had my first watsu with Walter, I explained my project and asked if he would let me interview him. I was particularly curious about his life choices, since I had never met a watsu practitioner and I wondered what circumstances had led him to this profession.

When I learned that Walter's father was never allowed to visit him after the divorce, I realized what a shock it must have been to read in the newspaper that his father had died. Shortly thereafter, Walter was using a Microsoft program and was hooked up to customer support. He heard the technician on the line say, "That's interesting. My last name is Wingo." As they chatted, Walter realized he was talking to someone who had the same father. In fact, he was talking to his half-sibling. When the two discovered this fact, they were amazed and delighted, like two Shakespeare characters finding out the hidden identity of their long-lost brothers or sisters. He also had a half-sister.

Actually, I was not at all amazed that this could happen," Walter said. "I do believe in fate. I look back and see my whole life was programmed since the fourth grade when I found a tie with a nude woman painted on it. I wore it to Sunday school. Now, I am ending my life as a watsu practitioner, surrounded by nude women in a heated pool."

"So, Walter, tell me now what it is that you want. Is this enough for you? To be surrounded by naked women in a heated pool?" I asked.

Walter then developed another theme: he was always looking for what he was missing. As a student at the University of Chicago and at Harvard, Walter was both bright and successful. After college, he had the good fortune to find a job on Madison Avenue as well as his first mentor, who got him promoted eventually to first vice-president of the corporation.

By twenty-seven, Walter had it all: a wife, a son, a house, and a great job. But then, the nagging question surfaced. Is this all there is?

Fortunately or unfortunately, Walter met Timothy Leary and began to experiment with drugs. After three tries, with his wife acting as a control group, Walter had his first LSD experience. He concluded during his drug-induced state that " God is a gas." He had sensed his own body as a gaseous substance and extrapolated from the experiment that he was God and that therefore God too was gas.

What followed was a lengthy journey of seeking and letting go: first of his wife and child, then of New York and Madison Avenue, then of conventional bourgeois life. Walter became a hippie looking for community. His journey took him via British Columbia to Harbin Hotsprings in northern California. Finally, Walter claimed, he had found his path to cosmic consciousness and the healing work he would devote himself to.

Walter's latest relationship was with a reflexologist who still loves him and is his best friend. When she and Walter split up after seven years together, Walter told me it was for her own good. She was excessively dependent on him. He was still suffering from their separation when he suddenly had a vision. He felt that he was his totem animal, the buffalo. A voice began to speak inside him and the voice said, "The heart of the buffalo is so strong, it cannot be broken." That is why Walter calls himself "Buffalo Heart."

I was not surprised to learn that Walter was a poet. Walter insisted that the threads of his life were coming together. He had recently reconciled with his son. He was trying to help his first wife who had been dumped a second time by Walter's good friend. Walter was beginning to create and build his own vision of community. In fact, he had met a group of women who were practicing the ancient art of Tantra. These women were helping him embrace more of his yin energy, which would eventually influence his yang energy.

"Most men are afraid of "yin," he said, "just as many are afraid of evil and other dark aspects of creation."

For Walter the secret was embracing it all.

As for what he wanted, Walter was not seeking a particular, concrete woman. He was looking for enlightenment, or more precisely an infusion of cosmic consciousness. He reminded me of Prometheus with a half-eaten liver, a punishment for stealing fire from the gods. But unlike Prometheus, Walter had found water where he played like a dolphin, emitting healing rays of energy.

MURRAY'S RESPONSE:

In talking to Murray about Walter's life and perspective, I found that I had been somewhat naive. Murray lived in California and had met many people like Walter who experimented with their lives. His assessment was that Walter's journey was both common and false. He then provided me with a synopsis on the American search for direct religious experience of the divine. He had no doubt that Walter wanted an authentic life and wanted to give up the Babbittry that undergirds all of American experience.

That search existed in Catholicism, in the Pentecostal traditions, among African Americans and the Shakers, Quakers, theosophists and mystical movements flourishing in the 60's. The movement in the sixties took two forms: an absorption of Eastern religion (ordinary but vulgarized Buddhism) or the tribal beliefs of native Americans (hence all the vision quests to discover totem animals).

Ordinary Buddhism with its precepts of right mind, right living, right work, etc. calls for a disciplined and painstaking set of principles that are extremely difficult to realize. Tantra, its philosophy and practice, far from being swift and easy, is a most difficult approach. It is referred to as the "short path" or the "diamond path." The Buddhist texts warn that anyone who tries it can go mad. It should not be undertaken without a guide. The results of doing it alone can be disastrous. It seemed to Murray that Walter could be in danger, that he was too fragmented, too limited, too uninformed, that many people in the tantric community were merely into "fucking," Not sending energy up the chakras for divine purposes.

I thanked Murray for this succinct illumination of all the journeys I had heard about, while in California. I realized I had been ambivalent and somewhat untrusting of Walter's story. But I am prone to believe in mysticism because of my father's search for "Peace of Mind."

I grew up with a father who believed in God. Recently, before going to California, I had dated a man from the eastern medical establishment, a doctor who liked me, but couldn't bear my poetic, imaginative, imagistic way of speaking. Both he and a colleague had treated the Dali Lama and their reports were totally antithetical. One, the report of my friend, was factual to a fault; the other was more literary and subjective. I decided to share this dating experience with Murray, to contrast my encounter with Walter, the watsu practitioner. What follows is the story of my love affair with a physician who had an overly developed left brain.

What do you think of Murray's reaction to Walter Wingo? Have you met anyone like Murray? Have you any interest in someone like Walter? What do you find attractive about either of these men? Which qualities turn you off?

XIII

"Sits he on never so high a throne, a man still sits on his bottom."

— Montaigne

Lionel, the doctor with an overly developed left-brain

Here is the story of Lionel. He's a professor of medicine and he has reached the top of a field, which requires a great deal of critical thinking. As you will see, he never shuts off his left-brain, which is constantly evaluating, criticizing and categorizing. He is not only successful in his field, but he is well connected and wealthy. Above all, he values his intelligence and he began our friendship by telling me: " I just want you to know I'm very bright. It's a description just like the one I've given for the color of my eyes or hair."

"That's all right. I'm very bright too," I replied.

And so we talked, two people over the phone, both in our sixties, both academic achievers, both Jewish and both looking for love.

"What do you look like?" he asked

"If you're looking for skinny, you can forget about me," I replied. "I'd say I am attractive but overweight."

"Are you pear-shaped," he asked.

I wasn't sure of his drift, so I told him I looked more like an apple.

"What about wrinkles?" he pursued.""I was almost in love with a Boston Brahmin, but she had too many wrinkles."

"No, I'm not wrinkled," I answered. I was beginning to feel like a racehorse with my mouth pried open to reveal my aging teeth."" I also have remarkably good teeth," I added.

" I like nice teeth," he answered. "Mine are too soft. I may need falsies some day."

I began to chuckle at the image of a man approaching me without teeth. I remembered how my mother looked and the strange sight of her dentures in a glass. How vulnerable she always seemed to be! "If I start loving you, I'll love you toothless," I said.

"First, you should know what I want, how I lead my life," he began and then proceeded to describe his routine.

"I eat Irish oatmeal for breakfast. Then I go to work, first to the hospital, then to the University. I come home at six .You should have dinner on the table exactly at 6 p.m. After dinner, which takes about an hour, I go to my study and write. This is my Monday-Friday schedule. My wife must be able to pursue her own interests from 6:30 to 11 p.m. At 11 p.m., we go to bed and make love."

"Every night?" I asked

"Every night," he replied.

"But what do you do for exercise," I asked.

"I avoid it. The only exercise I get is from what I do in bed."

" I love to walk. Would you consider walking with me for thirty minutes?" I asked straightforwardly.

"On the days we walk, there will be no sex."

"But doctors recommend walking. They even suggest it increases vitality."

"Who listens to doctors?" was his unexpected, sardonic comment.

After this initial conversation, he sent me a 38-page resume. I sent him some poems. He insisted that I recite them to him over the phone. I agreed to read him one or two a night. He said he'd be coming back on Sunday, after a medical convention in Chicago. He wanted to take me out for dinner; I could choose the restaurant.

"Just be ready at 5:39," he stated with authority.

I gave him directions to my house and immediately called some friends we had in common. One was a doctor at the same hospital with this new Lothario. My friend said that Lionel was indeed an outstanding doctor. As for his personal life, my friend knew he was divorced and had two children. He thought we might get along well because Lionel was""brilliant." I mentioned that he had already informed me how""bright" he was.

"Is there anything really negative about him?" I asked.

"The only obvious weakness is that he still smokes."

"Cigarettes?" I exclaimed." But he's a doctor!"

"Yes, it's paradoxical. But I'm certain he has a rationalization. He can sometimes be very hard on other doctors."

Perhaps he'll give it up, I thought, seeing myself rescuing this man from potential lung cancer. Naturally the first topic of conversation on our date was smoking. This topic irritated him and he retaliated with, "You're pretty, but you need to lose weight between your pubis and your rib cage."

When I finally saw his apartment, it was orderly and clean, high ceilinged with a large pantry. He certainly was not living in squalor. There was little to no carpeting, however, and his furniture looked like the stuff I had in college. There was one china cabinet, probably from his mother, which housed a lot of crystal. The paintings on the walls were distinctive. His brother was an abstract painter, a rather impressive painter at that.

He took out *The Joy of Cooking* and began to prepare spaghetti. He was obviously as precise in cooking as he was in practicing medicine. We ate in his spacious kitchen. I felt comfortable, at home. My trust level was high. I had thought about the position I was in and I had prepared a little speech about wanting to wait until I got to know him better, if he were to make a pass. I knew he had a long hard day and so had I. I would have to leave early to go to work the next day.

After dinner he said, "Let's sit on the couch and neck a little." "Necking" was what my generation did in the forties and fifties. You didn't go all the way. You sat in automobiles and kissed a lot, and sometimes you let a guy touch your legs or your breasts. But you always stopped before things could get out of hand. He told me he liked me a lot, that he was thinking about me a lot. But characteristic of his pattern, he became witty and guileful. " I would think you'd like to check me out, given what you've told me about your past. Don't worry that I'll think badly of you in the morning. I am not moralistic about sex. Besides, we're different. You feel at ease when you're talking. I need to get closer to you as though we were in bed.................."

All the right thoughts went through my head. I shouldn't have come here. It's too soon. I don't know him. He doesn't know me. I pushed him gently away and started to rise from the couch. Suddenly he rose and put his arms around me and pleaded for a chance to see if the chemistry would work between us. He was surprisingly strong and even though I resisted, I became dizzy with desire and fear. If I were younger and virginal, I'd call it something like a date rape. But I was sixty-four. So I called it the beginning of a love affair. He was seriously smitten. He invited his children to meet me, which, for most men, is a sign of commitment.

I am a sucker for flowers. I am also a sucker for brilliant men. He was that, apparently. And during the course of our affair, he diagnosed my undiagnosed diabetes and my son's rashes and my friends' ailments. He was extremely well connected and we flew hither and yon while he collected honorary degrees and made speeches. I began to imagine what it would be like to live with him. I wasn't sure that we would continue to be compatible because he was often extremely critical of me. I had the seven deadlies before I could count to ten. His major criticism was that I couldn't communicate (i.e. communicate as he did—). What he objected to most was my verbosity over the telephone.

Lionel said one day, " I'm going to describe a person two ways. I want to know which description you prefer. First description. There was a woman named Mrs. D. who baby-sat when my parents went out. Second description. A woman, named Mrs. D, who wore a red hat and had peonies in her garden, used to baby-sit for us when my parents went out. Now which description do you prefer?"

"The second one, of course, "I answered. "It has images. I can see her."

"I prefer the first. "Nothing but the facts." That was his penchant.

He also objected to my health consciousness. Not only did he smoke five cigarettes daily, but also he kept pirogues in the freezer and didn't think twice about eating fat, marbleized meat. When I told him that the raw egg whites in meringue destroyed vitamin C, ("fact" I had picked up from Adele Davis in the fifties) he looked at me with outrage and disgust.

"Don't ever say anything like that in front of my medical friends," he shouted in the super market. "I would be embarrassed by your ignorance."

Eventually there was a crisis. We were invited to have cocktails with someone Lionel had not seen for ten years. They had a major disagreement and their differences of opinion still rankled. Lionel still respected his friend and was nervous about the reunion.

On the way, he explained the relationship he had once had with this friend and how the friendship had ended in misunderstanding. It turned out that this friend had a son who was writing poetry. It was also surprising that his friend and I collected works by the same potter. He and his wife invited us for supper and instead of leaving after the cocktail hour, we left at midnight, having had a wonderful evening.

As we got into the car, Lionel yelled at me. I knew something was up because he had kicked me under the table several times. When I asked what the matter was, he began to rave.

"You interrupted me five times. Did you know you interrupted me five times?"

"You're lucky it wasn't seven," I answered, laughing at the discrepancy between his depression and my elation.

"Besides, you're missing the point. We had a great evening and you're now reconciled with your friend. He liked me. They asked us to stay for dinner. They liked me."

"You wanna bet? They were just being polite. They just felt sorry for you. You try to sell yourself too much."

This irrational criticism hit me hard. I had just discovered that I had diabetes. The last thing I needed was a devastating analysis of my weak points. I felt unloved. We were staying in a bed and breakfast. I packed my bags immediately at midnight and drove back to Hartford.

I guess it was a shock to his fragile ego, which was large but not invincible. I admit that I contributed to the demise of this relationship. I had formulated a rule that I would be with people who uplifted my spirits and eliminate people who brought me down. Lionel was too much of a perfectionist to uplift anyone. This Pygmalion destroyed rather than created his ideal woman.

I thought about Lionel for several months and I concluded that he lacked imagination. He was a brilliant physician, factual and objective, but he couldn't possibly feel what others feel. In some respects, he was surprisingly insecure. Perhaps the root cause was his Jewishness. In a society full of prejudice, he had climbed the ladder to its top rung, but he hid his sense of inferiority under arrogance, dogma and a narrow band of responses in the "supermensch" category. I recalled that he had yelled at a cab driver who was making us late for a ceremony. When I mentioned how rude he was, he scoffed, "I'm in the upper classes. You're supposed to yell at servants who don't perform properly."

You are wondering, Murray, why I went out with him? I must confess I was taken in by his status. And you told me that I saw men as artichokes, rough on the outside but gorgeous inside. I suppose that I thought of Lionel as the largest artichoke I had ever seen."

"Well, I fully understand, Minerva. You did have moments of unity with this man. But he is not really intelligent. All of the intelligent men I have known have been kind."

Murray then commented that most of the men I had described to him seemed to be pretty exotic.

"Did you interview any ordinary ones, nice guys, run-of-the-mill guys? Forget about the watsu practitioners, and architects and super professors." I replied to Murray that indeed I had interviewed many "ordinary guys " and I would send him an Email with their profiles. I warned him that it might make for dull reading.

"But perhaps your readers will want such men," Murray said wisely.

So I sent him the following stories about Steve and Gary.

XIV

"To live and be joyless is sinful."
                                    – Anonymous

Steve: a company man

There are a great many widowers who have adjusted to being single. They've accepted the household chores and their lives are as structured as they want them to be. They've had reasonably good marriages, and they're enjoying their freedom and independence. They like to ski or do some other sport seriously. They are not particularly interested in younger women. They enjoy traveling by themselves and they don't really want to marry again.

Such a man was Steve, an employee of a large steel plant. Steve had moved around a great deal as a young boy. He read a lot, was a bit sulky and shy, had no deep friendships. When he married, it was to a secretary of a medical director. He had one son who was currently getting a divorce. His son had two children, grand daughters whom he saw rarely. He explained that the son was like him, didn't care that much about money. The divorce was what the wife wanted because she had been dissatisfied with a husband without financial ambition.

Steve admitted he was looking for a companion, a woman with a good disposition, someone who was generally cheerful and optimistic, not depressed. "No night clubbers or drinkers, or political activists. I'm looking for a person who can adjust to rain pouring down on our picnic."

His dead wife had been his best friend." She had put up with a lot," he acknowledged. " I was in an audio-visual group and I was away from home about 129 days a year. My wife never complained. We both loved nature and the outdoors. We drove to all the national parks in the US. When I took up skiing, she never criticized me for buying all that fancy equipment."

"When she died the wheels fell off the circus wagon. She had breast cancer. I dreamt about her a lot, but I just knew a chapter in my life had ended. I wasn't going to sit around, idling like an engine. So I've been dating women, but I'm disappointed. I've found they aren't really interested in me. They always talk about the times they had with their husbands. Most of them had children who have had children. They're very involved with their families. They've forgotten their husbands were rats. And they keep subsidizing the children and their children.

In fact, one of these women I've gone out with a lot gave so much money to her kids, she herself is hurting. She just couldn't say no. The other thing she did that I disliked was to listen to TV preachers. She kept telling me the end was coming.

But she did play a damned good Scrabble game. We had a good time together, but we stopped seeing each other because her kids got in the way. The phone was always ringing. The daughter called for advice about her husband. The son called to hit her up for more money."

I finally asked my provocative question: You say you couldn't care less about money. Were you a generous husband or were you a bit stingy?

Steve replied, "I haven't experienced any problems with money, even though I have to admit that as I grow older, money begins to pinch. But I have a neighbor who is preoccupied with numbers. He's really a tight wad. His wife wants to go to Europe. I told him he should take Mary to Europe and he said,'"She can go to the library and look at the books.'"

Steve remembered when his neighbor was participating in the Boy Scouts and they were all supposed to bring food for a party. He remembered that his wife had made a casserole and his stingy neighbor had brought a loaf of bread.

My reaction to Steve was that he was a bit tiresome and more detached than I felt was healthy. There are many men out there like him. I guessed that he was idealizing the wife who never complained. There was a hint of guilt when he spoke of her, as if he might have contributed to her death with those 129 nights spent elsewhere.

But, basically, Steve was a nice guy who had loved his wife and cared about his son. He might be interested in marrying again if he found a woman who could be cheerful.

Note to Murray:

So, what do you think of Steve, Murray? Or did you stop reading? If not, here's another one, a nice guy named Gary.

XV

"Only the old, the tried, is safe; or so it seems."
— *To Have Or To Be*

— Erich Fromm

Gary: safe in a gated community

The photo showed a nice-looking guy dressed in a white sweatshirt. He said he was 67 with a background in computer science. He was 5' 11" and weighed 175 lbs. He was a software engineer before he retired and he was currently living in north Florida in a gated community. He had traveled only in the US and had been single approximately ten years. He had two wives and one daughter with each wife. I found him exceedingly difficult to draw out.

"I guess I'm shy. I keep my mouth shut a lot. I don't like to offend women. I never criticize them. Everybody's different. Everybody's entitled to their opinions."

When I asked him if he had changed as a result of his two divorces, he said his character hadn't changed at all. In fact, his first requirement was that he wanted to meet a woman with integrity. He couldn't stand liars. Both of his wives had lied to him. That's the reason he left.

He was looking for someone to travel with. He had called a number of women who were members of "Single Adventurous Voyageurs."

"It's my fault I haven't found anyone. Somehow, I never follow through. If I meet them, I never call them back for a second date. If I like them over the phone, I don't make a date. And I don't like aggressive women who take the initiative. I really can't explain it. Things just don't work out."

He sees his daughters occasionally. They live up in the DC area. He doesn't talk to his ex-wives. Why should he? All they want to do is argue with him.

What he does like is photography. He got very enthusiastic when he talked about Santa Fe and the Albuquerque Museum. He had taken many photographs when he was in New Mexico and his major source of pride was a photography show of his work at the local Florida Elks Club House. His biggest dream was going to Australia without any time restriction. He wanted to find an intelligent, non-smoking, attractive, reliable woman who had good manners and enough money to share the travel expenses. Someone between 40 and 63.

I told him I was sure that such women exist if he would just move a little, get out of his gated community and let down the wall that was protecting him. I explained that I experienced his perplexity as fear, that I thought he was too fearful of being hurt. After all, there are many single women in Florida looking for a predictable man, not exciting, not terribly adventuresome, but safe and timid and easy to influence.

Murrary's response to Steve and Gary:

I see your dilemma, Minerva. These are men who became numb long ago. Their souls have shrunk. But there are lots of fearful women who might like the companionship of guys like Steve and Gary. For you and me, I agree, send more neurotics and eccentrics. Send only the juicy ones.

I answered Murray with the following tales of Thomas and Lester:

XVI

"Paradise is people who are not boring."

– Fay Weldon

Thomas: a disabled playwright

"It all began with my mother," he said. " She was great, a beauty who made the best chocolate cake I've ever devoured. She had large green eyes, big breasts, and arms like a large envelope. My father was famous. I kid you not. He won a Pulitzer for ————. I have never been able to live up to his expectations. But I've had a rather interesting life—rich in romantic attachments: comedy, tragedy, tragi-comedy, comic-tragedy..."

"Hold it," I interrupted. "Can you give me some facts? Where have you lived? How many wives have you had? Do you have children?"

"I'm glad to oblige but,... I'd rather tell you about me my way. I've written plays and I know how to weave a tale."

"O.K. You go ahead," I conceded. And he did for hours and hours.

Thomas was born under the sign of Woody Allen. In Manhattan, of course. He had moved about so much as an adult that he made the wandering minstrel look like a couch potato. He had lived in Texas, Illinois, California, Colorado, Massachusetts, Connecticut, Washington, DC, Missouri and Delaware. His work life included teaching drama and creative writing, acting in summer theater, being a public information officer, running an ad agency, serving in the US Army, winning political campaigns and writing plays and short stories.

He had three wives and five kids. All of them were scattered about the world. He didn't see any of them much.

His second wife tried to commit suicide with sleeping pills. He was away from home on a political campaign. He hinted that he was having an affair with a woman who loved politics as he did. He referred to his insatiable need for oral sex, which his first and second wives did not enjoy. His romantic escapades rivaled those of Don Juan and he was more than happy to tell me about them.

The tragedies in his life included marrying the sister of a woman he truly loved (a spin-off from the Bible story about Leah and Rachel). She became pregnant (the sister) and he did the right thing. He also had a horrendous car accident, which had reduced him to his current Proustian state, a stationary, indoor solitary, staring out of the window.

"I was traveling across a bridge in San Francisco and a car came at me from the opposite direction going 105. It hit my car squarely and my car somersaulted, turning me upside down. I landed on my head and was hospitalized for six months. The final diagnosis was epilepsy. The only good thing about my stay in the hospital was that I had an affair with the head nurse. Right now, I'm suffering from a broken ankle that won't heal. So I don't get around much anymore."

He began humming that tune ("Don't Get Around Much Anymore"). And then he injected a warning," If I stop talking to you suddenly, it's because some neighbor is knocking at my door. I'm living on welfare, as are several others in my apartment house. The women like to nurture me and they're always dropping by with a casserole or something good to eat. Then they expect me to be their midnight snack. I've gained so much weight, I'll probably burst and die of obesity. They're driving me mad. It's such a relief talking to you. You're far away. You're unattainable. You're my ideal romantic partner."

I felt sympathetic, not because he was humorous (a quality I value highly), but because I understood the "up and down" movement of those who seek fame and fortune and end up down and out. After several hours of listening to his complete autobiography, I did try to extricate myself. "Thomas, it's been a pleasure talking to you."

But he couldn't let go of my ear. He began breathing heavily. I thought he was having an epileptic seizure. There was finally silence and then a moan, a low animal-like moan. Then he spoke.

"Please give me your phone number. I have a lot more to tell you, and I love your voice, your laughter. Perhaps you'll let me tickle your fancy. We'll discuss literature and film. O.K.? I want to know all about you."

I tend to be overly empathic. After all, he was helpless and lived far away. He was also the funniest man I had interviewed. As it turned out, I did enjoy our conversations, his flirtatiousness, his upbeat stories, " in spite of my judgment of failure." He was like Boethius in prison. But instead of writing a "Consolation of Philosophy," he was weaving Scheherazade tales to keep me enthralled. Eventually I sent him my poetry book.

The next week he called to tell me he was walking and the first place he went to was his local bar where he read my poetry aloud to all the people in the establishment.

"They loved your poems," he said, beginning to recite several of them by heart.""They want you to come down here and do a reading in the bar," he added. "It's a great group. They loved the fact that your poems are so accessible. One of the women started to cry when I read the poem about your dead husband, "My Self, My Husband, and the Blue Balloon." I even read that one to the married gal who visits me on Thursdays."

He then began reading my poems with such deep and responsible understanding; I knew I had found a true "appreciator."

I can't categorize this man. He was such a mixture of paradoxical traits. Yes, he's an appreciator and a creator. But he's a big-time loser financially. Yes, he is well read, intelligent, generous and open. But he is a proud and boastful womanizer. He is immoral and amoral sexually, but he doesn't pity himself. And even though he is a wounded man (with a bad leg), he is somehow mythic, like a fisher king, waiting for someone not just to heal him but also to heal the land where many are living in helpless defeat. He is more like Robin Williams than Woody, seductively whimsical and free-associational, witty and weird, like a child whose mother had given up on toilet training and preferred using diapers for the rest of his youth.

———————

How do you feel about Thomas? Do you find him interesting? Do you feel like rescuing him from his isolation? I think I felt touched by him.

Murray's Response: Minerva, once again I have to remind you that you are on shaky ground when you use words like "rescue." Did you ever work for the Red Cross? Here's my take on your Thomas.

Negatives:

1. He married his first wife because she was pregnant, even though he was in love with her sister. What a complicated plot.

2. His second wife tried to commit suicide with sleeping pills. He admits he was having an affair with a camp follower during a political campaign.

3. When he was hospitalized, he had an affair with the head nurse. That's like Clinton and Monica in the Oval Office.

4. He is currently sleeping with a married woman who comes to his apartment on Thursdays.

5.   He was probably masturbating while he talked to you, not having an epileptic seizure.

6.   His metaphor for life is an oral one of "eating," from his mother's chocolate cake to the breasts of all the women in his world.

7.   He's a lousy father. He never sees his kids.

Extenuating Circumstances

1.   He did marry the woman whom he impregnated.

2.   He's got a lot of libido and is very playful.

3.   The married woman who comes on Thursdays probably isn't getting enough enjoyment at home. She has a money-grubbing, boring husband who's cold and a lousy lover.

4.   He does have epilepsy and that is a terrible disease.

5.   Most men do love oral sex after sixty.

    I would recommend this man to a very savvy woman who's not afraid of catching herpes or syphilis or even AIDS. He wants to laugh a little, cry a little. Otherwise, he's a sad case.

XVII

"Of all the famous men who ever lived, the one I would most like to have been was Socrates. Not just because he was a great thinker, because I have been known to have some reasonably profound insights myself, although mine invariably revolve round a Swedish airline stewardess and some handcuffs."

– Woody Allen

Lester: A Jewish jester

One of my neighbors suggested that I interview a friend of his. He guaranteed that I would be entertained by his endless repertoire of jokes. My neighbor swore that he was a man of outstanding integrity, one of the 36 anonymous saints, a "tzadick" (wise man), and one who supports the world with his goodness. Such high praise smacked of hyperbole. I knew if I swallowed it, I'd be disappointed. But I proceeded to make a luncheon date with Lester, the Jewish Jester, at my favorite Chinese restaurant, the Cheng Du.

Lester showed up looking much older than I had expected. He admitted he was 79. His bent frame suggested osteoporosis. However, he dressed nattily in an arty silk shirt and light woolen slacks, a fashionable dandy. This man had taught history. That's why he began to talk about his parents right away. They had come from Russia. His father had been a wigmaker for the Moscow Arts Company. When he arrived in this country, he became a barber. His mother's father was a shoe merchant. That probably inspired Lester to become a high fashion shoe salesman. Even though he spent his childhood in a southern state, he later moved to a northern locale where he was influenced by an excellent school system. He excelled in mathematics and started an underground newspaper during high school.

"The principal was a martinet. He promised to make a number of reforms and then he proceeded to screw us."

This incident was formative, in that Lester subsequently spent a good part of his career fighting for the rights of teachers. He was the president of a union for many, many years.

Lester returned to the tale of his childhood, asserting that he had loved both of his parents. They never pressured him. Once when he came home with a "C" on his report card, no one raised an eyebrow. After high school, he attended a prestigious university where he met his first wife-to-be. They were happy for 10 years and had two sons.

67

Unfortunately she died of lung cancer. His eyes teared up and he confessed he still missed her. However, he met and married another woman who turned out to be an alcoholic. They divorced after fifteen years.

Then he met the woman of his dreams, a woman with whom he had a grand "amour." He kept referring to her as his "schicksela." They met in the union, both of them on a negotiating committee. She ended up winning a wage increase of $11,000. She owed him. So he asked her to have dinner with him. They immediately fell in love, the kind of love that expressed itself in swoons and the wish to be next to each other till eternity.

Two years before this interview, when they were on vacation, Lester suffered a convulsion. He was diagnosed as an epileptic. At first, the "shicksela" stuck by him, assuring him she would never push his wheel chair over a cliff.

But then, one day, she began to think about her future. She was considerably younger. "I may not be marketable in five years," she explained. So much for their concept of eternity.

Lester did not seem to be bitter. In fact he said he still included her in his will. He also luckily had two sons and lots of grandchildren. The biggest problem in his life, he said, was that he had night blindness and couldn't drive to the many movie theaters he loved. In the course of our three-hour lunch, he interspersed remarks about his life, literature, and the pursuit of happiness, with jokes that came from a bottomless repertoire. I've included some of his "bons mots" in the following list.

1.   As a union organizer, his main job was to get the unappreciated to unite.

2.   He gave a lot of advice: Never talk when the cash register is open. Never try to snow a snowman. Don't sleep on the job unless you're a mattress tester. Always dress better than the boss to show you don't need his money. Never pray for a new king.

3.   He knew a great many truisms, such as: The fast nickel is better than a slow dime. Every country gets the Jews it deserves. Chutzpah pays. Life is like a cup of tea (Don't ask why).

4.   It was from Lester that I first heard the joke about when life begins. There's a Catholic priest who says life begins at conception; a Protestant minister who says life begins at birth; and a Rabbi who says life begins when the kids are in college and the dog dies.

Needless to say, Lester was a delightful and entertaining "mensch." My neighbor had been right. I enjoyed this interview immensely. But I was struck by the totally opposite reaction I had to my interview with Thomas. In some ways, they were similar. Both of them admitted to being interested in large breasts. Both adored their mothers. Both were humorous and preoccupied with finding love. But Lester was truly an honest, hardworking, committed adult. His emphasis was on meaning. He said at the end of a serious discussion of Durrell and Philip Larkin, cynicism and hope, that for as long as he lived, he had no capacity for withdrawing from "engagement."

I decided that Lester was on the path to wisdom. He has transcended his limitations. But I think he's in for a shock. His friends and family are not in the same city. Women are not going to drive him to the movies, not the kind of women he wants. He is interesting and intelligent and reasonably funny, but many older women shy away from men with handicaps, just as many older men prefer younger, healthy women. A lot of people are looking for caregivers and many do not want to be the givers of care. I know that sounds a bit cynical, but I'm trying to be realistic. Recently Lester sent me a book of his late wife's poetry with a note that said he had decided to write a book about his years of union organizing. I applauded his self-reliance and was glad he had found more purpose in his life.

In a sense, Lester is one of the happiest men because he had found passion late in life. He still has all his marbles and he is a man who knows his own depths. He's not a superficial clod or dilettante who thinks too much about himself.

How do you feel about getting involved with a man who is sick or has some disability? An interesting personality and a sense of humor are extremely desirable qualities. Even if a man is disabled, he can still be a wonderful person to do things with.

XVIII

"Since the marketing man has no deep attachment to himself or to others, he does not care, in any deep sense of the word, not because he is selfish but because his relations to others and to himself are so thin."

– Erich Fromm

Leo: a marketing Everyone

Some men do fit the stereotype of what single men 60+ are looking for. Leo was one of them. Even though he was 74, he wanted a woman 45-50. He had never finished college and had spent his professional life in an advertising agency and in a real estate brokerage firm. He was of Italian descent, he stated, 5' 8," weighing 170 lbs. His wife had died five years ago of heart disease related to diabetes. She had also been a heavy smoker.

At first he found it difficult to live alone, but he adjusted quickly and now he feels satisfied with his singlehood. He never wants to marry again. "If I had a wife in the house, I probably couldn't watch my sports programs and sleep with the TV on. I like noise all the time."

When I asked about relationships since his wife's death, he said he was extremely interested in women. In fact, he has a best friend whom he has known for three years. At first, they had a'"sexual" thing, but that had ended. He still cares about her. As a matter of fact, just as I called he was on his way to her gift shop so that she could go to the doctor.

"We understand each other," he continued. " I'm stable financially. She isn't. She needs to put two kids through college. So I help her a little. We go to Atlantic City together. But I basically do my own thing. I'm mostly on the up and up with her. But I don't mention that I go out with other women. She had two bad marriages and she's had surgery for a disease of the lungs. No point in hurting her feelings. I'm healthy. I've done weight training every day of my life. I love to dance. I'm in great shape. I like cruises. I like having freedom and lots of space."

"Would you call yourself a good time Charlie? I asked. " A good guy out for a good time. No strings. No commitments. "

"Yeah, I guess you could say that. But I've raised my family— two boys, and I've got two grandchildren, six and nine. I don't need to take on any more kids. The trouble with most women is they want a guy who'll be a husband and a father. It's not realistic. Guys my age just want to find a sexy gal. I like the big-breasted ones, but they have to be short—around 5' 4" weighing 120 pounds. Not scrawny. More like Gina Lollobrigida. Somebody who likes to cuddle. Somebody with a good sense of humor. Her weight should be proportional to her height. Hey! How about you? Do you ever come to New York? I go in all the time to see musicals. "My Fair Lady." "The Music Man." I'll show you a good time. You sound like my kinda girl, sexy. Are you interested in a world cruise? Do you like to dance?"

I said politely I'd call him if I decided to come to New York, knowing full well that I never would. I couldn't stand a man who needs noise all the time. I love silence, bird song, night noises. I have met or talked to five men who play the TV all night long. Is it loneliness? Is it a fear of their own dark dreams? What does it do to their brain waves? I suppose if it were Baroque music, I could accept it. Such music starts your Alpha waves and facilitates creative thoughts. But just noise from TV? Ugh! Torture! Living hell!

Most of my friends would not be interested in meeting this man because they would find his behavior toward his lady friend dishonest. But I'm sure there are women who would enjoy a "good-time Charlie." He's a kind of swashbuckler, a Romeo without any depth. You might not meet him in church, but you could find him in Gold's gym, for sure.

I believe that Leo is a prototype. They are out there. They are available.

> Now, I want to turn to another type of man who does join dating services, especially services like "Single Wordsmiths." *That type of man has never married.* In most cases they have answers as to why they never married. But the answers are diverse. Again, there were individual differences and life experiences which determined their choices, It was never just "men who avoid commitment." Are they all problematic? Would you, my reader, entertain the possibility that some are not?

XIV

"We live, not as we wish to, but as we can."

– Meander

Mitchell, the Mensan, who wanted "thin."

Mitch is 71 and single. *He has never married.* He is tall, he says, and thin (six feet one and 168 lbs). He is a psychotherapist with a lot of impressive degrees. He works with brain-damaged children.

He joined "Single Wordsmiths," but he'd like to find a woman to travel with around the world. He specifically wants someone fit, slim, bouncy, and danceable, curious, a good conversationalist who could pay her own way.

Given my weakness for men who dance, I did not interview him without ulterior motives. When I asked him why he had never married, he said he didn't want to inflict himself on another person. He came from a highly dysfunctional family. His siblings had married and were all divorced. He had no intention of hurting himself or another by trying to do what none of his siblings could do.

However, he had been involved, both short and long term, with another psychotherapist for 29 years. "We were good together. She was a wonderful dancer, a creative, nurturing, bright lady. She only weighed 103 pounds."

"What happened?" I asked, eager to hear the ending.

"Well," she announced one day, "Mitch! I have to stop seeing you. You give me bad dreams."

His voice cracked over the telephone. He sounded so melancholy, I felt nothing but compassion.

"I knew I was her father substitute, a protector. Maybe she didn't need me anymore. It's been a year and a half and I still miss her terribly," he began to sob.

After a respectful pause, I asked what he was doing about his great loss, his feelings of rejection and abandonment.

"I've gone out with a number of women, but they turn out to be 'Jewish American Princesses'."

"Please define that term," I asked, knowing that this man was not Jewish.

"That's a woman who says only one word: GIMME, GIMME, GIMME. What she mostly wants is...money. Not sex."

"Are you a particularly generous man?" I asked. "Many men I've spoken to are very 'frugal' or parsimonious'."

"Don't, please, compare me to other men. Did I tell you I belong to Mensa? You do know what Mensa is, don't you?"

"Yes, of course, it's an elitist organization for people with high I.Q.'s. Since you're a member, why haven't you looked for a Mensan woman?"

"They're all fat!" he asserted.

"What do you consider fat?" I asked.

"Oh, a woman who is 5'6" and weighs over 150 lbs.," he replied quickly.

"Whoops!" I said. "That's my weight and height."

Despite his condemnation of fat women, I continued to chat with him. I recommended a book by Dr. Irvin Yalom, *Love's Executioner*. Yalom, a friend of mine, explores his own revulsion toward fat women. "At least he admits it," I said, "roots it in his ambivalence toward a corpulent sister and mother."

"I know Yalom's work. I like his book on group therapy. But I don't think he's on the right track with his fiction. He confesses too much. He's too personal, too eager to show how fragile and vulnerable he is. I can't stand all this mea culpa "I-too-am-human" stuff. We've got presidents baring their souls and their genitals. We've got women baring their breasts and their underbellies. I wish we'd go back a bit to privacy and discretion. As for my desire for thin women, it is not the formlessness I have an aversion to. It's the overt symbol of a lack of discipline. I don't like people who are stupid or undisciplined."

I was getting uncomfortable talking about this subject, so I asked Mitch if he ever reads poetry. He responded by quoting some of his poems. To my surprise, they were turgid and sententious, flowery and bloated, not at all what I would have expected, from a disciplined, thin man.

Would you be more comfortable with a man who is as critical and demanding as Mitchell? Is dancing important to you? How do you feel about men who cannot stand "fat" women?

XX   A SECOND MAN WHO HAD NEVER MARRIED

"Everyone is a moon and has a dark side
Which he never shows to anyone."
                                    – Mark Twain

Jimmy, A social worker who loved "goodness."

"I love goodness," Jimmy told me. "Generosity of spirit."

Jimmy was a handsome man with blue, soulful eyes. He was in his late fifties and had never married. We were on a plane flying to San Francisco. Somehow we started talking about what we did and when Jimmy discovered I was writing a book about single men over sixty, he confessed he was sixty-one and very much single. He was a social worker in a school system and he said he didn't have an opportunity to meet many single women.

This was his first trip to San Francisco. He had spent all of his other vacations in France or Italy. He was going to San Francisco alone. He knew no one there. It was a departure from his usual trips, which involved peace- making attempts. He belonged to an organization that was worldwide. Their mission was to promote peace. He had lots of experiences staying in the homes of people who belonged to the same organization. And usually, he told me blushingly, he would find a beautiful woman, a French or Italian woman and have a brief affair.

Always these women had high ideals. They were committed to working for peace. He had met many in the sixties like that, but there were still many left who cared about non-violence, about the environment, about a world that would be safe, without war.

"Is there anything else that attracts you in a person?" I asked.

"Well, language is important to me. Perhaps too important. I read a great deal. I write poetry. I want to find someone who is playful and expressive. I like women who are high-spirited, unconventional, and even defiant of propriety. But they have to love to serve, love to do good deeds, love to give to others.

"Have you ever been in love?" I ask.

"Once, yes, in graduate school. But she had a boyfriend. Maybe I'm afraid of failing, of being rejected."

"Or maybe you're afraid of realizing your dream," I injected.

"Well, I think I'm ready to settle down now."

"I actually know someone who meets your criteria and she is French and speaks that language fluently. Would you be interested in meeting her?" I asked.

"Is she thin?" Jimmy responded.

"Why does she have to be thin?" I asked.

"Well, I'm never attracted to overweight women," he answered.

Shades of Mitchell. Yet another one obsessed by thinness. I wished him well, but I had a feeling this social worker needed some therapy. Yes, he had a rich, fantasy life. Yes, he was attractive and sensitive and idealistic.

Yes, he was sweet and "good." But deep inside, the ghost of Oedipus still stalked him. I doubt that he will ever be ready to marry.

XXI   A THIRD MAN WHO HAS NEVER MARRIED

"First, prepare you to be sorry
That you never knew till now,
Either whom to love, or how."

— Ben Jonson

Milton, a librarian, who wants a larger social network

The stereotypic view of men over sixty is that they all want pretty women. Attractiveness comes first. The personal ads stress thinness ("petite" or "slim"). They all seem to be looking for doll-like women, delicate, feminine beauties whom they can parade as trophies or think of as angels in their houses. I decided to go to a luncheon in New York that was sponsored by "Single Wordsmiths." I asked the people in charge if I could interview men after the program and they agreed to make an announcement. At least ten men stayed to talk to me. Some stayed for quite a while waiting their turn.

Perhaps it was the sample. Perhaps it was the fact that many of these men were intellectuals. They were all avid readers. None of them mentioned that they were looking for pretty women. Most of them stressed intelligence. They added to intelligence a list of qualities such as caring, enthusiastic, easy-going, happy, nurturing, energetic, warm, etc. Some of them mentioned thinness. But thinness was mentioned with health, not necessarily attractiveness.

A great majority of them sounded disillusioned. They did not sound hopeful that they could find someone right to put in their pumpkin shells.

At the end of interviewing nine men, an older man approached me. He was probably close to eighty. He looked a little like Bob Hope in his declining years. There was a twinkle, a quizzical expression, a need to say something entertaining, to amuse. He talked freely about his life.

"These guys you've been talking to are younger than I am. Ask me what I want? I just want to wake up every day, want to be alive. That is enough of a triumph."

He told me he had been a librarian for forty years. He had never married, had never had children, had no relatives, and had been in retirement for fifteen years, and read voraciously. He took long walks every day, swam at the YMCA, and took guitar lessons. He did watch a lot of television. Occasionally he went out with some woman whom he thought might be interesting. Usually not much happened.

"Are you still interested in sex?" I asked, wanting to find out more about his life-long commitment to non-commitment.

"Of course," he bellowed. "What man isn't? Women always want a relationship. Men want sex with anyone. I don't really care how she looks, so long as her equipment is there. I think if I lived in the country, I'd make out with a cow or a sheep. It's hard to find such connections in Brooklyn, although I've known some women who could pass for cows. What about you, honey?" he asked, patting me on the arm. I gave him a cold look and continued the interview.

"Can you tell me anything about your life that has made you so cautious about marrying or having children? Are you a voracious reader because you can't relate well to people or are you unable to relate because you live in books all the time? Which came first, the books or the inability to connect with people?"

"First of all, I think I connect with people when I'm reading books. Sometimes these people are more real to me than the people I meet. Second, there's nothing very different about my childhood. My parents were immigrants, Jewish immigrants. My father had a tailor shop. My mother helped him. I was an only child. I read a lot and I was a pretty good student. I didn't play sports, though. I did best at marbles and tidily winks. I did have a girlfriend in high school. She was Chinese. I love the way oriental women look. I wanted to marry her. My father and mother came down on me hard. "You will not marry a goy!" they said. "You will not have a child who has a Chinese mother."

I don't know why I broke off my relationship and listened to them. I was a pretty docile adolescent. When I went to City College, I was a studious young man. We didn't have much money, so I worked at night doing odd jobs: soda jerk, janitor, and, finally, bookstore clerk. I loved working in that bookstore and I decided that being a librarian would suit me just fine. Books are not just my friends, my world. They are everything for me. When I'm immersed in a book, I'm the happiest I can get. So I guess I decided to marry books and forget about people. Besides, in the books I read, nothing ever works out well. Look at *Anna Karenina.* Look at *Madame Bovary.* Look at *Gone With the Wind.*"

"Well, what about movies and happy endings? What about comedies? What about "living happily ever after?" I countered.

"What about death? Now we're talking reality. What about dying alone? What about all the bodies they find ten days later after they've died in my apartment building? They're stinking, rotting. They have to knock down the door to get in. I don't want to die like that. I want somebody to care whether I live or die."

"So that's your bottom line. That's what you want. A woman or a person to care whether you live or die."

"What's wrong with that? It's a modest request."

"What's wrong is that you don't want to <u>be</u> a person who cares whether someone else lives or dies, do you?"

"What makes you say that?"

"Well, all I've heard from you is that you can't find anyone who suits you and you're worried that you'll die alone."

"Yeah, I guess I do sound like that. But I'm really a good guy. I always try to be entertaining when I take women out."

"Do you pay the bill?" I asked boldly, not explaining why I asked that question.

"Yeah, I always pick up the check, even if I don't have much money."

"Well, I would have thought that such generosity would be appreciated by women. I've met a lot of men who are using the new "enlightened," liberated ethos to stop paying for dates, letting everyone go Dutch. Have you ever taken out a woman who has more money than you do?" I asked.

"Well, if they ever did, they kept the secret well-hidden," Milton answered.

"I've enjoyed talking to you, Milton. I hope I haven't been too tough. I think you've been truthful about your love of life and your fear of death and dying alone. It's true that you need more of a social network. You should have a companion, if you really want one. There must be a woman out there who would appreciate your point of view, which is not romantic, but speaks of basic human needs. If I were you, I'd try giving more, getting involved more, joining more groups. I know that runs counter to your reclusive, bookish temperament, but in the end, you'll prefer human flesh to words on paper. Best of luck."

Do you know any men who have never married? Do you disagree with me, that such men are poor bets for long-term relationships?

XXII

"Anger is a weed; Hate is the tree."
— St. Augustine
*"A woman has got to love a bad man once or twice in her
life, to be thankful for a good one."*
— Marjorie Kinnan Rawlings

Charles: an angry environmentalist who has recently divorced

Yes, I did talk to some men who made my spine crawl. I also dated a man whom I had known for years and discovered that he was a sadistic, arrogant bastard. My parting words to him were:

"You are a regression in my evolutionary spiral." I had enough experiences with leaving and letting go or being left and being let go of, that I had gained the wisdom to know it is not a good thing to vent your anger and disappointment in violent words. In part, I had recognized that it was my mistake that I had woven a net of goodness over these men. I did not really know them. They were figments of my imagination, my need to idealize.

But you are longing to hear who these men are. What are they like? Some of you are saying, "I told you so. That's why I don't bother going out anymore."

The last thing I want to do is reinforce your fears. But I have to be honest with you. There are men whom you definitely should avoid. Perhaps you won't agree with me. That's fine. If you see a prince where I see a toad or a serpent, to each his own.

Interview with Charles:

"I'm at peace with my body, soul and mind," said Charles.

"I eat one meal a day. I have two drinks every day. I don't eat sugar or fat. I've lost 25 pounds and I'm in harmony with my circadian rhythms. I live five minutes from my boat. In other words, I own my life. That's what divorce has done for me," stated Charles forcefully with total conviction." When you marry, you give away your life. The best $7,500 I've ever spent was on my divorce lawyer. All I got from my marriage was a pita."

"What's a pita?" I asked, confused by his conclusion.

"A royal pain in the ass," he answered without hesitation.

"Let me explain," he continued. "I can go to Molly's on Route 2. It's a strip joint. I can look at naked women any time I want to. And you know what I ask myself?"

"No. I honestly don't," I muttered, realizing this man had a story I shouldn't interrupt.

"I ask myself: Is this why they fought the Trojan War? Women are dogs or dumb or both. That's my assessment. You marry a skinny one. She gets fat. I'm over six feet. I run every day. I'm in great shape. Do you think my wife ever ran? Do you think she took care of herself? Do you think she ever owned up to her responsibilities? Never."

"Owning your own life is of inestimable value," he concluded with a flourish.

Charles told me he was romantic, wealthy, healthy and wise (or at least well-informed). He subscribes to 50 periodicals. In addition, he has used his energy and wealth for certain causes he cares about. He was an organizer of a major environmental movement. He is socially conscious, attractive and theoretically still interested in women, despite his words of angry rejection. He says he goes to singles groups in his area and he is actually looking for a traditional woman who has old-fashioned values. In fact, he became specific and confessed that he liked petite Asian women. They know their place. They understand what it takes to please a man. Old-fashioned Asian women, of course.

Before I hung up the phone, I asked him if he would listen to an interview I had written about another man who wanted a woman with old-fashioned values. I explained to him that this man, like him, was angry still at his first wife who had divorced him, that he was not as intelligent or healthy or strong-minded as Charles, but there were certain similarities: anger, a denigration of women and a desire for a traditional woman who could cook, i.e. be subservient and accommodating like an Asian woman.

"Sure, I'll listen. But he doesn't sound like me at all," said Charles. "I've got my shit together. I like my life."

"I'm merely suggesting that you're both pretty angry and you're blaming your ex-wives and you're coming to the same conclusions," I repeated.

"O.K. Go ahead and read. I'll listen, even if it's a waste of my time," said Charles.

XXIII

*"A Liar is a crooked gun, that carries wrong, and his bore is
a great deal too big for his bullet. He has a natural antipathy
to Truth, as some have to cheese and cats."*

— Samuel Butler

Stephan: the wolf in grandfather clothing

I was vacationing in Florida and decided to call a few men who lived in
the general vicinity. I flipped through my profiles and picked someone who
looked very handsome and who was holding two adorable grandchildren on
his knees. He said he was looking for someone to travel with. He claimed he
was fit, financially secure and ready for adventures. He would travel anywhere
in the world with the right person. Everything about him on his profile page
exuded kindness, goodness, sweetness and light.

When I called him on the phone, he immediately told me he'd like to
take me to lunch. I declined. But he said that he would cooperate and be
interviewed if I would consider having dinner with him. I said I'd like to
interview him first before I made such a decision. So we began to talk.

Stephan was born in New York. He was of Polish descent and a graduate
of a fine college and had a good business involving health spas. He loved
women, he told me, and spent most of his time in the company of women.
He had a housekeeper who was a woman and a live-in masseuse who gave him
massages every night. He had made lots of money and was focusing on enjoying
life.

He had been divorced for twenty-five years and had paid twenty-five years
of alimony. The only time he had dealings with his ex-wife was when she went
after him for more money. It had not been an amicable dissolution. In fact, he
was angry at that very moment because his daughter was siding with her mother
against him. The two children in the picture were his daughter's children. He
was furious with his daughter and was not speaking to her. She had refused to
let him see his grandchildren.

He admitted that he had been an alcoholic. He said that his alcoholism
had contributed to his divorce. But he had stopped drinking in the eighties
and was absolutely on the wagon permanently.

I asked him about his romantic life since his divorce. He said, "In the
seventies, it was easy to get laid. All you had to do was give a girl some
marijuana." He had many girlfriends in the seventies, beautiful girls, and young

girls. He kept telling me what a good guy he really was. In fact, in the early eighties he said he had become a born-again Christian. That's when he stopped drinking.

"How did your romantic life change?" I asked, thinking that some pure, puritanical answer would emerge, that he had limited his list of girlfriends or had given up sex entirely or had discovered massage and preferred it to sex.

"I started using prostitutes," he answered. "I usually see prostitutes three times a week. I also have a good thing going with my housekeeper, a woman who hasn't been with a man for many years. I pay her well," he insisted. "She likes it."

By this time I was beginning to recover from my dropped jaw. "What about your live-in masseuse?" I asked

"Oh, I screw her occasionally too. But it's funny. She's strong but she's not firm enough. If I'm paying, I like 'em firm."

"And your employees?" I asked.

"Yeah, some of them are the best. But when I want really good sex, I use prostitutes."

I could hardly keep myself from hanging up the phone. I began to lecture him. "Do you know that prostitutes carry AIDS? And that the highest incidence of heterosexual AIDS in this country is right where you live?

"No shit!" he exclaimed

"Have you ever been tested for AIDS?" I asked.

"Hell, no," he said.

"I'm going to tell you a secret. I've got cancer. I didn't tell you that or put it in my profile cause I figured it was a turn-off. But I'm losing all my teeth from the chemo. I'm still good-looking. And I'm a good guy. I don't worry about AIDS cause I've got cancer."

I knew already that logical thinking was not one of his strengths. But I pursued his illogic with a question," If you found out that you had AIDS, would you tell your women about it?"

"Well, I don't know. I like to tell little white lies. When they ask me what I'm doing about sex, being single and all that, I just say I masturbate a lot."

It was time for me to end the interview. So I said, " Can you sum up in a few words what it is that you want in a relationship?"

"I really love women. And I'm a good guy. Did I tell you I help out in the hospital? I feed cancer patients lunch. I cheer them up and I smile at them. I know it sounds like I go after the wrong women, but the truth is I'd like to find a traditional woman, someone who likes to cook. I'm not sure they exist any more. Do you think there's someone like that who would put up with me?"

Conversation with Charles:

" So what do you think of this man, Charles? His anger and his denigration of all women?"

"I think he's an s.o.b. He's not like me. Sure, we're both mad about our ex wives. Women can be pretty mercenary. But I would not stoop to such a level to go to prostitutes. I told you I'm a wholesome guy. I care about myself. I take care of myself. This guy is a real creep. He's dangerous. You should call the dating service and get him off the list. I don't want to be in an organization that has people like him in it," Charles added.

"I did call," I explained, "but the owner said that Stephan was just pulling my leg. He felt sorry for him because he had cancer. He wouldn't remove him."

"Well, give me his name and I'll call," Charles said.

"I'm sorry; I can't do that," I replied.

I remembered that I had told all the people I interviewed that our conversations would be disguised enough so that they could not be recognized, that I would be fictionalizing them. So, I decided not to reveal Stephan's name, but to tell his story, so that women would be cautious about the men they talk to in'"Single Adventurous Voyageurs."

XXIV

"The desire to experience union with others manifests itself in the lowest kind of behavior, in acts of sadism and destruction, as well as in the highest solidarity on the basis of an ideal or conviction."

– Erich Fromm

Peter, the peeping Tom

I hope you never meet the man I'm going to describe. Peter was looking for someone to travel with to Athens, someone between 45 and 65. He said he was short, 5' 7" and weighed 147 pounds. His photo revealed a smiling face, definitely pleasant, boyish, disarmingly open. He was interested in history and had been an academic before his one big heart attack. Retired to a sunny climate, he sounded like a good catch.

He confessed that his first wife was unhappy with his academic salary.

"I gave her the opportunity to increase her wealth by releasing her from our marriage vows after ten years."

I was feeling sympathy for him, knowing how emasculating that complaint from a wife can be.

"I hope she's living in Donald Trump's apartment house. We had two sons together. They tell me she has breast cancer. She has not remarried."

When I asked him about his childhood, he said it had been normal, that he had played on the basketball team in high school. His worst complaint was that he had flat feet and could never become a star.

His second wife came from Costa Rica. She was a surgeon. She had a son who was eighteen.

"During our marriage," he said, "she gained fifty pounds, got high blood pressure, skin cancer and breast cancer. In addition, she complained about the size of my penis. She had other complaints as well. She never could stand the suburbs. Her son refused to go to school and she let him stay home. Finally, when I became impotent, I gave her an airline ticket and sent her back to San Jose. I had offered to fix her up with a functioning man. I did all I could. But she refused all my creative solutions.

I met my third wife at a scientific meeting. I met her at a bar in Houston. She was half Jewish. Her mother had raised her as a Protestant. She visited me in New York. I took her to good restaurants and we watched the Mets play. She had a sixteen-year-old son who seemed to be all right. We got married. She was great at oral sex. She would go down on me every time I wanted it. We were getting along fine. In fact, she understood me better than any woman I had known. She never diminished me. She didn't think I was smarter than she was and when I had my periods of impotence, she and I agreed she should see other men."

All of this information came out in a great rush—a monologue, which I dutifully recorded. I had little time to think. I didn't ask questions or comment. Finally I interrupted him.

" You said you had a happy childhood. But your sexual tastes seem a bit....."(I struggled for the right word. I didn't want to offend him. "Kinky?" No "Perverse?" Definitely no.) Finally, I came up with""unusual."

"Oh, I forgot to tell you that my mother would go down on me when I was 10, 11, and 12. I came from a wealthy family and my mother was the one with money. I guess I've accepted her domination. I like being controlled by women. I even like being hurt by them."

I paused and thought liberal thoughts. No wonder he is so screwed up. No wonder he keeps getting divorced.

"Have you tried psychiatry?" I asked, always the little helper.

"No," he replied.""But I did date a psychologist and she liked to fuck two men at the same time. Her second preference was screwing another guy and letting me watch. She actually taught at the University of Chicago. When I made her, I would pretend to be Mack, the president of Sloan Kettering. She loved it."

· "Are you still married to her?" I asked, knowing that the answer would be no.

"No. We got divorced. I found a Spanish woman who asked me to join her on the Riviera. For some reason I can't understand, my wife couldn't dig two gals and a man. She just liked two guys and a gal. She tried to commit suicide. So I had to leave her."

"Do you have anything further to tell me?" I asked, hoping to end the interview.

"Yeah, I guess you'd like this. Once we went to a porn film together. We found a guy and brought him home. He proceeded to rob us both. But that's enough about me. What about you? I've been candid. Tell me about your story. Who are you hanging out with?"

"No one," I answered quickly. I had just broken up with Ernie.

"Well, aren't you going to tell me about your life, your latest loves?"

"Oh, my life is pretty conventional. I usually break up with a man when I feel he has stopped loving me."

"I bet you're always doing that. You've probably made a mistake. Tell me about your last lover. Was he good?"

" I really don't think it's appropriate for me to discuss my life."

"Hey, that's not fair. I might have some good advice for you. I think you should call him back and say you made a mistake. Then I think you should see him and hop into the sack. Afterwards, you should call me up and tell me all about it."

At that point, I hung up the phone and went to the bathroom to wash my hands. I felt a little sick. Luckily I went swimming and washed my soul clean in the night sea. I called the dating service that had supplied Peter's profile and again I complained that they should screen their clients. This time the owner said that I didn't understand people, that there were lots of people who were into that kind of sex. Just because I wasn't into it, I shouldn't be condemning others.

What do you think of this response to my concern? Are you as turned off by Charles and Stephan and Peter as I was? Do you consider them dangerous? Or are you someone who likes "that kind of sex?" Why did I include these men? To provide a warning to those of you who do not believe there are such dangerous men out there.

In a recent survey (November, 2003) in the AARP Magazine, it was noted that The Center for Disease Control reported deaths from AIDS had been declining, except in the 45-64 year old category in which AIDS is spreading more quickly. My fears are not unfounded.

Nor is sexual dysfunction unusual. Dr. David Schnarch is quoted in this survey as claiming that 1 in 2 men over 45 is sexually dysfunctional and that such a condition is natural, This last statistic should be of interest to any woman who thinks that she will find a man over sixty who will have the potency of a young lover.

Beware! But don't stop looking! Perhaps the solution for you will be a younger man!

XXV

"Not every man into your household bring,
For offering shelter is a ticklish thing."

      – King Solomon in *The Prologue to The Cook's Tale*

Willy, the tape bamboozler

When I returned to Hartford, I found a message on my answering machine. "This is William Von der Weden. I have your profile from "The Best and the Brightest." I would like to meet you. I will send you a letter with more detail."

He spoke with an accent. Needless to say, I waited for the letter with some curiosity. It came with a box of Dutch chocolates. Enclosed was a picture of a white-haired man, sturdy, stolid, cherubic like Santa Claus. He was moving toward a soccer ball, about to kick it. He explained in his letter that he had been a professor of astronomy, that he came from Holland and that his wife had died recently of Lou Gehrig's disease. He would be visiting his son and daughter-in-law in Ohio and it would be convenient to meet me after leaving them.

I was still seeing Ernie and was uninterested in meeting another man. I wrote him back and said so. He responded that he was merely trying to make friends, that he would respect sincerely my wishes to be platonic.

"Couldn't you receive me as a colleague who wants to visit Cape Cod?"

He had seen in my profile that I had a house at Cape Cod and he wondered if I went up to it in the fall. He was hoping to visit the Marconi site.

I wrote back that I was extremely busy. He called to try to define how busy. I admitted that I was going to the Cape for Thanksgiving with friends and my son. He said he liked to play soccer.

Perhaps my son would like to play with him on the beach. It just so happens that my son loves soccer. And the guests I had invited included a man who was on the football team at Dartmouth in my husband's class. "Well, it might be nice to have two soccer players invite my son to play with them." I said.

Finally, after several phone calls and discussions, I told him he could be my guest for Thanksgiving. But he had to accept that there would be no romance at all, no overtures, no attempts. We decided he would stay in a motel in Hartford for one night and then we would drive to the Cape: my son, William and I.

I met him at the airport and he handed me a gift from his state to mine. Three heads of lettuce.

"Fresh," he said, "absolutely fresh."

Odd, I thought, but I said thank you as if I had never received nicer gifts. After I gave him lunch and he ate most of the Gouda I had bought for the weekend, we went for a walk around the reservoir with one of my friends, Cyndy. Cyndy found William quite charming, full of stories about growing up in Holland, full of information about flora and fauna and stars and constellations.

"It might be nice to fix William up with Astrid," said Cyndy. "You know Astrid, Minerva. She's Dutch. You'll be back from the Cape by Saturday. I'll invite them both for dinner."

We then made arrangements for William to rent a car on our return from the Cape so that he could go to Cyndy's for dinner. Things were shaping up. I would only have William as a guest for a few nights and I was looking forward to a men's soccer championship game.

The only problem was the weather. It poured. Instead of playing soccer, we sat around playing Monopoly.

William passed out all sorts of gifts to my other guests: seafood forks and marigold seeds and videos of the National Parks—all the prizes he had won opening bank accounts. He gave me an enameled black tray with a gold Star of David on it. The most appropriate gift was a soccer ball to my son. The next day it stopped raining. Between massive amounts of food, we took walks and William regaled us with stories about his family and experiences he had since his wife's death. He told us he was puzzled because his second son no longer welcomed him as a visitor. It had to do with the fact that he mentioned something about sex in front of his thirteen year old grandson.

When we were alone, I began to interview him about women he had dated since his wife's death. The stories followed a pattern: always the relationships terminated with a fight; the women left him in anger. William was perpetually puzzled as to why. One woman had a seriously wounded shoulder and William inadvertently put his arm around her in a movie theater. She screamed. Later in the car she poured hot coffee on him and left him by jumping out of the car.

Another woman he met through the dating service invited him to be a guest in her house. He claimed that she asked him to leave after he asked her about her monogrammed silver and its worth. A third story involved a woman he had known in Holland when he was a boy. She lived in Hawaii and both he and his wife had remained friends with her. When he visited her in Hawaii, she had only one bed and they had to share it. But she put a large board between them and he had to agree not to touch her. He agreed with the arrangement but somehow, during the night, his hand touched her by mistake, he said. She threw him out the next day.

Something mysterious seemed to happen in all these cases. William couldn't explain these endings. On the way back to Hartford, William suddenly announced, "Minerva, I have a deal for you."

My ears perked up. His language, the use of "deal", startled me. It was not a word I used, except pejoratively.

"I'd like to sell you a second mortgage on my house," he continued.

"Do I look like a bank?" I replied. "Why would you suggest such a deal?"

"Well, you're such a generous person, I thought it would be good to be in debt to you," replied William.

"William, stop talking this way," I emphatically stated. I could hear my son coughing in the back seat of the car. He was getting anxious. William then changed the subject, while inserting a Chopin tape into the tape player.

"Would you like to have my Chopin tape?" was his next question.

"No. Thanks, but no. It's your tape." I again couldn't fathom why he was asking me this.

"I thought we might have a tape exchange. I took the liberty of putting your "Loyko" tape in my suitcase and I thought———."

"You did **what?**" I shouted.

I drove the car off the highway and stopped. (This "Loyko" tape was precious to me. I had bought it in Edinburgh at the Fringe Festival. It was recorded by a group of Siberian gypsy singers. It could not have been replaced.)

"Please open your suitcase and get my tape," I commanded imperiously.

William went back to the trunk and opened it, found the tape and handed it to me sheepishly. I gave him his Chopin tape and drove back in absolute silence. I couldn't wait to drop him at his motel and then call Cyndy and Astrid. They did not cancel the dinner. But they reported the next day that he had eaten them out of house and home.

During the evening, William learned that Astrid was going to Europe, but she hadn't bought her ticket yet. He suggested that she buy it on his credit card so that he could get the frequent flier miles. Astrid did not have a credit card that gave her such miles.

Postscript

Did I hear from him again? Of course. He called to ask me what he had done that angered me so much. I wouldn't speak to him. He couldn't understand my reaction. He had a wonderful time and would like to be my friend.

It's a year later. I am typing his story. Again, last week, William called to say he would be at Cape Cod and would like to take me out for dinner. His message did not acknowledge that I haven't spoken to him since the aborted tape theft. He seems to deny not only what happened in the past, but also his own contribution that brings about his bizarre situations.

> Do you think I was silly to invite Willy to my house? Would you be able to risk meeting such an odd man? Or would you chalk it up to an adventure that netted a story you could laugh about for many months? Of course, I'm not suggesting you shouldn't be careful. You should generally meet new people whom you don't know in a crowded place. Watch out for inconsistencies in their stories. Don't let them take you home, etc. But there are exceptions. And in this case, Willy was harmless.

XXVI

"Nay, if you come to that, Sir, have not the wisest of men
in all ages, not excepting Solomon himself—have they not had
their Hobby Horses, their running horses, their coins and their
cockle shells, their drums and their trumpets, their fiddlers, their
pallets, their maggots and their butterflies."

– Lawrence Sterne, *Tristram Shandy*

Wayne: a real estate agent in search of class.

Wayne told me right away he knew what he wanted, a woman with class. In fact, he insisted on E-mailing me a definition of what he considered class to be. A rose crawled up one side of the page that read:

- Class never runs scared. It is <u>surefooted</u> and confident in that knowledge that you can meet life head on.
- Class never makes excuses. It takes it's lumps and learns from past mistakes.
- Class is considerate of others.
- Class has a sense of humor. It knows that a good laugh is the best lubricant for oiling the machinery of human relations
- Class bespeaks aristacracy that has nothing to do with ancestry or money.
- Class never tries to build itself up by tearing others down.
- Class is real. You can't fake it. If you have class you don't need much of anything else. If you don't have it, I don't want you.

The six pictures that Wayne included in his profile showed a man dancing in a white tuxedo with black trim on the lapels and pockets. The woman he was dancing with looked "glitzy," a look that Wayne told me later he especially loved.

Another photo showed the large, diesel motor home he owned, covered with painted scenes of mountains and sunsets and a silhouetted couple dancing. He had joined "Single Adventurous Voyagers" at least a year and a half ago. He was looking for a fun-loving, happy, healthy, secure and sincere class lady. To show his adventurous spirit, he included pictures of himself on an African Safari, in an Air Force helmet and on a large, white horse. The most prominent picture showed him on a dance cruise wearing a white leather suit. He was financially secure as a real estate developer. In addition, he was absolutely healthy, having parachuted off mountains, water rafted, snorkeled in the Caribbean and flown around the Arctic Circle.

He was definitely a woman's man, he said. "I'm not one of the good, old boys. I prefer the company of women." He described himself as a loner. However, he had married once and stayed married for fifteen years. He then admitted that he had married her because she was a great real estate agent.

" I told her to find me the best apartment in town and she did. So I married her."

He had two children from that marriage and the children had two children. Unfortunately, the wife became a closet alcoholic. Since they lived in the same town and belonged to the same country club, they had an arrangement that she would go to the club on Tuesdays and Sundays and he would go on Mondays, Wednesdays and Saturdays. Thursdays and Fridays the club was closed.

He was still griping that his ex-wife had walked away with a diamond that was worth $18,000.

He had almost married a second time. He met this wife-to-be while managing one of his properties. She had a waterbed in her apartment above his office. The ceiling began to leak water. He went upstairs and knocked on the door and this fantastic knockout of a woman opened it.

After giving her many massages over a number of weeks, he decided to marry her. But he wanted a pre-nuptial agreement. Her mother came along and raised such a fuss, inspired by greed, that he broke off the engagement.

I asked him why he never tried again. He replied," I guess I'm looking for mountain tops and not valleys."

When I probed further, it turned out that he didn't want to grow old by himself and he was getting a little tired of women who could jump off mountains, young ones who could not relate to his kind of life style.

"You see, the young ones can wear blue jeans and look at home, but they can't wear a gown and be comfortable at the Captain's table. Now, you sound more like the kind of gal I've been looking for. You know I'm a generous man. I just sent six dozen roses to ladies I like. You know, I take my women to Las Vegas and we stay at the best hotels. I pick up the tabs for everything. I buy clothes for my women and we go to a few shows. All I ask is that she be a mountaintop and not a valley. Sometimes I can get moody and I guess I'm kind of selfish. But I'm a generous man, a very generous man."

I suppose you could say, "This man has his own style." But it wasn't my style. I wouldn't like Las Vegas. I wouldn't like his white leather suits. I wouldn't like his motor home covered with paintings out of a Disney movie. I wouldn't like the fact that he misspelled or misused several words in his list on class. Call me a social snob. This man's definition of class seemed a bit preposterous.

But he had good intentions and, unlike many of the men I had met or talked to, he was undoubtedly generous.

"Thank you for talking to me, Wayne. If I come across anyone who looks like a mountain top, I will give her your name and I wish you the best," I said, wondering for a fleeting moment if I could ever be a woman who wanted to be taken care of by an American cowboy. But I've been there. I've done that. I know those days are over. I not only can be, but I also want to be my own caregiver, my own van driver, and my own class act.

Wayne has many fine qualities. Perhaps I'm being a bit of a snob. Does he appeal to you at all? If so, why? He did have an optimistic personality. And he is not stingy. What else did you like?

XXVII

"One of the most striking differences between a cat
and a lie is that a cat has only nine lives."

– Mark Twain

Rex: a dancing doctor with a youthful mind

How can I classify **Rex,** a physician and a free thinker? His profile from "The Best and the Brightest" indicated that he had been married three times, that he reads historical novels, and that he loves the ballet and the theater. His definition of a good relationship was impeccable: respect, physical attraction, common interests, the desire to share, etc. She should be optimistic, honest, healthy, emotionally and financially stable, 5ft. 3" to 5ft. 9," non-obese, non-alcoholic, non-drug-addicted. He claimed that what he had to offer was love, love, love and loyalty. He wanted to share a full and interesting life based on an equal relationship. He said he was 68.

The photograph attached to the questionnaire was that of a young, healthy, bronzed, alert, blonde man in a short-sleeved shirt holding what looked like ski poles. He appeared to be fit as a fiddle- head- fern emerging in spring. Wonder of wonders, he also loved to dance.

I was going to be in his neck of the woods, so I called to interview him. I thought I might find a dancing partner for one evening, someone who has been absent from my life. We agreed to meet at a vegetarian restaurant (his choice). I had sent him my picture and I already had his. But when I entered the restaurant, he wasn't there. After looking around for five minutes, I spotted a man who had not moved from the receptionist's podium. He looked a bit like a dapper movie star named Adolph Monjou. He was wearing a three-piece suit. He looked very fragile and VERY old.

That was Rex. I thought he trembled as the waiter guided us to our table. IMMEDIATELY HE TOLD ME HE HAD LIED ABOUT HIS AGE, that he was 79, not 68. "Why did you do that?" I asked, still astonished. "Well, if I had said I was 79, would you have called me?" He told me that, indeed, he lived as though he had eternal youth, still skiing, dancing, and hiking.

I thought to myself that he was right; I probably would not have called him.

"Are you still practicing medicine?" I asked,

"Yes, of course, but I take off at least one day a week to ski. In fact, I just drove to ——and skied for five hours and drove back. That's not what 79 year olds do."

There were lots of other surprises in the evening as well. I learned more about his three wives, particularly the last one of the three. In answer to my question about what had happened to break them up, he replied, "She told me she felt like a second class citizen. She was always jealous of the time I spent with my four sons, "splendid chaps," who live in different states in the US. I very much enjoy seeing them. I took her with me once and it spoiled my fun. She's what you Americans call a "couch potato." Never does anything athletic."

But the main reason for the divorce was her tardiness, he confessed.

"We were always late for everything. She's South American and she dawdles over her makeup. It was infuriating, especially when we had tickets to the opera."

His other two wives were also South American. In fact, he was looking for another South American woman. He came from Australia.

"But you didn't say that in your profile," I mentioned.

I remembered a man I had once known named Donald who had married three times women named "Lois." Whether he thought she was Lois Lane and he was Superman, Donald was caught up in dreams of an ideal.

Rex had a similar obsession. But he was an extraordinary man, well traveled, highly educated, and alive both physically and mentally. He had roots in England, loved Anglican churches, and still was excited about practicing medicine at 79.

We had a delightful evening, so delightful that we didn't go dancing, but instead we talked and talked. At midnight I took a cab back to my hotel and Rex said, in parting," I'd be happy to see you even though you're not South American. You are a vibrant lady with wonderful high energy. That's what I like, really."

Footnote:

Rex was not a boring man. He was humorous, intelligent, charming and interesting because of the mechanical nature of his fixed ideas. Henri Bergson's definition of the comic was "the mechanical encrusted on the living." In a way, Rex reminded me of the mechanical Bluebeard who kept putting his wives into closets. He was not scary, however. He might be difficult to live with, but he would certainly be an interesting date, entertaining and sui generis.

Would you have felt about Rex as I did? Would you have overlooked his lie? Would you have found him charming and debonair and entertaining. How do you feel about his pattern of marriages? Do you know anyone who keeps marrying a certain type of woman again and again?

XXVIII

"What a chimera then is man! What a novelty! What a monster, what chaos, what a contradiction, what a prodigy! Judge of all things, feeble earthworm, depository of truth, a sink of uncertainty and error, the glory and the shame of the universe."

– Pascal

Moses, an electronics expert, seeking a woman with a scientific mind

During the summer of 1997, I called men who lived all over the country. I wanted to have lots of geographical and professional diversity. As for ethnic or economic diversity, I had a hard time finding that. The men who joined these dating services were mostly white, middle to upper middle class, educated through college and interesting enough to attract my attention. Obviously, the process of joining a dating service separates people who don't have money from people who do. But I kept looking for variety in other ways.

When I called Moses, I ended up with an individual who was totally different. He had grown up in Brooklyn, but had spent his adult life in Texas. He told me right away he was looking for a woman with a scientific mind. He was tired of humanists, he said. He could follow their conversation, but they could never enter his world. His passion was machines, his profession, electronic engineering. All of this was significant information along with what he had written on his "Single Wordsmith" profile page.

He had owned his own company, he said, but now he was retired and indulging himself reading biographies. He was hot on the Bell Curve, which he had used as an approach to any aspect of human endeavor. I am particularly weak on scientific information, so it was all I could do to follow him through his maze of statistical observations. I did, however, find him to be open about his relationships, and his one marriage which had ended in divorce a good many years ago. He admitted that he had been somewhat of a neglectful husband during the twenty-five years he had been married. His wife did not have a college degree. But she was very bright and a good mother and now she's married to someone who is just right for her.

"Why didn't you remarry?" I asked.

"Because I can't find a woman with a scientific mind. I don't care so much now about sex. I'm looking for an intellectual companion who wants to keep learning and sharing. I have a lot of ideas I'd like to talk to someone about. For example, there's a fallacy I'm interested in, that you can't be objective and emotional at the same time. Listening to Bach can bring tears to my eyes, not romantic tears, but rather tears of appreciation for the mathematical structures that are being revealed."

Even though I listened to him with interest, I found that he was a bit odd. His eccentricities included driving only motorcycles, driving the motorcycles from Texas to Michigan or California, living in an apartment, while owning a house filled with obsolete machines, holding on to rooms full of data which he knew would be worthwhile some day, etc. Therefore, it was without regret that I ended the conversation, saying," If I come across a woman with a scientific mind, I'll send her to you."

To my astonishment, he subsequently found my E-mail address in one of his directories and began sending me analyses of the biographies he was reading.

"I hope you don't think I'm invading your privacy," he wrote, "but I enjoyed our conversation so much, I'd like to continue talking to you."

Before I could answer him, there was another long letter, reviewing yet another book. These letters were interesting and his approach to literary works was far different from my own. I've been trained in literary criticism and I always write objectively, including references and footnotes to prove my points. He wrote quite subjectively and personally, relating everything to his own life.

He called in September to ask me if he could come up to visit me. I replied that it wasn't promising, since I was still dating Ernie and since Moses had said he would only come up by motorcycle. I couldn't imagine someone spending two days driving to my house, visiting a few days, and then driving back on a motorcycle. It sounded a bit crazy for a man who was 75. I said no. He stopped writing. But at Christmas he sent me roses and in January he called when I had the flu. I was terribly sick, thought I would die, aches and pains and no boyfriend. Ernie and I had split.

Moses kept calling. He said he'd come up to visit and take care of me. I said no. He persisted. A friend of mine was coming in early February to stay with me for five days. I told Moses he could visit during that time, but he'd have to stay in a motel or hotel. He had said in a letter to me that for some men and women a long-term relationship hinges on sex. For Moses, it did not. It hinges on close friendship. He just wanted to be my friend. He said he would fly, rather than drive his motorcycle. The weather might be nasty in February.

When I picked him up at the airport, instead of finding a man who looked like Arthur Miller (the photo he had sent), there was a very old man with a short white beard looking like one of the seven dwarfs with osteoporosis. He was wearing overalls and a pointed felt green hat. I guessed it was Moses because the curvature of his spine suggested he had ridden too many motorcycles. I was disappointed.

However, we had a splendid week with Marilyn, who was there promoting her book. She and I had grown up together and she was intent upon convincing me that Moses was a fascinating man, terribly articulate and intelligent, knowledgeable about everything from black holes to how to make colonial furniture. She urged me to give him a chance. She even went so far as to say that if her husband were to die, she might be interested in Moses.

That did it. I decided to overcome my initial distaste for his exterior and focus on our two minds meeting. By March, Moses had come back and forth enough times and we had exchanged enough E-mails and phone conversations so that we decided to meet in Anguilla, my favorite island in the Caribbean. Moses warned me that his traveling days were over, but he would make an exception. He also warned me that he didn't like boats.

When we met in St. Martin, we had to take a ferry over to Anguilla. The sea was a bit rough. Moses did look as green as his hat. And then, in Anguilla, we rented a car. One has to drive on the left side of the road, British style. I suggested that I do the driving for a few days, until he became familiar with the island.

After a half day of me driving, Moses was so nervous that he insisted on controlling our wheels. He and I did have a pleasant time for a few days, reading books and walking on the beach. But he didn't like to swim and he didn't really like the sun and he never got excited about the landscape and he didn't dance very well. The greatest annoyance was that he arose each morning at 6A.M. to make himself a breakfast of oatmeal, peanut butter and cashews, all mooched together. I am a late riser and the tinkling of his cooking equipment at that ridiculously early hour inevitably woke me up.

Since my enjoyment in the Caribbean depends upon the landscape, I was happy. But after a few days, Moses complained of a bellyache. He stopped eating and groaned constantly. We had to leave the island early because he was in such pain. We flew back through Boston and I wanted him to see my doctor, but he refused. He wanted to go back to Texas and see his own doctor whom he could trust. I put him on the plane to Texas, worried that he might not make it home.

I received a bouquet of roses, but no phone call or E-mail. I waited and waited; worried that he had been operated on. I imagined that the doctor had opened his abdomen and found a Tootsie Roll of undigested oatmeal, peanut butter and cashews. Finally he returned my calls.

"Didn't you get my letter?" he asked.

"No, and I've been worried sick. Are you all right? What was the matter with you?"

"I'm all right now. But it was frightening. I'll send you an E-mail to explain it all."

The E-mail came.

"Your driving blocked my colon," it began."I know this to be true," he continued, "because of a motorcycle accident many years ago when I was almost killed. It was someone else's fault. My colon was blocked for a long time."

I sent him an E-mail response. "I didn't know I had so much power. Maybe they should put me on the Jay Leno show. **Minerva, the incredible colon-blocker.** Maybe, they could sell me as a substitute for lomotil."

I knew he was a mechanical man and relatively humorless, but I laughed because it all seemed so obviously absurd. He had also included in his E-mail a number of other critical comments: Like Lionel, he saw only the seven deadlies.

First, of course, I didn't have a scientific mind. " All you ever see is beauty," he wrote." I can't stand your ignorance of what is all around you. You have no scientific awareness. You do not understand how I see the world. What's more," he continued, "you are much too much interested in what you eat. Even though you are overweight, you didn't let one plate of bread pass you by. You lack self-discipline. I told you I didn't like boats and water. You were insensitive to my pain. In addition, you are far too gregarious for my taste. You even had a good time at the hotel cocktail party. You talked to everyone. I cannot think that we could ever live together. You are much too much of an egotist. However, I love you as much as I am capable of loving anyone and, therefore, I suggest we meet again in Washington, DC where there is a subway. I will never let you drive a car with me in it again."

He then listed all the reasons we should remain friends. They included the fact that we were both readers, that he had considerable knowledge of scientific phenomena that I didn't, that I had literary knowledge that he valued and wanted, that we were equally good conversationalists, etc.

Needless to say, I did not answer his Email. I saw clearly that I had found a man who overvalued machines. He was experiencing me as someone who was stripping his gears and then laughing at him. So much for men who have heads, but do not know the location of their hearts.

POSTSCRIPT

After my second volume of poetry was published in the fall of 1999, I sent out notices to a few men I had dated. I hesitated to send one to Moses. But I thought he might enjoy my book. So I sent him the information about the book's availability. He bought two of them and was most excited about my successful publication. He sent the following letter as well, telling me about his current romantic relationships. I've edited it to reveal more about Moses and his aspirations:

Dear Minerva,

I hope your personal life is a happy one. Have you found a partner? After we split, I went into depression for awhile (but not caused by you, although I do not rule you out as a factor). A thorough physical exam showed no physical causes. Then a lady on the west coast (an ex-biologist) and I got serious, and we visited each other several times. We've had our ups and downs, but our association is mostly up. Recently, life's suddenly become complicated, because Leslie, who had been my significant other for many years but who had left town to return to her origins, suddenly decided she wanted me back.

The concept of love has always puzzled me, but it seems so clear to most other people. I'm not able to bond as others do, and one of the ways this manifests itself is I'm not jealous when my lover pays attention to someone else. Intimacy in communication is more important in a friendship than the sexual aspect. It didn't used to be that way, but age has cooled my ardor. Intimate friendship with one person needn't and shouldn't close the door to others. So, after much pondering, I decided I wanted both women, and sent the same letter to both of them. My justification follows:

1. Monogamy is an evolutionary trait that ensures the welfare of the child until it can cope alone. In the early millennia of Homo Sapiens, the life span didn't go much beyond the child-bearing years, but it does now.

2. After the childbearing years, the drive for monogamy stems from personal choice and society's mores. In the animal kingdom, we see the gamut ranging from promiscuity at one extreme to monogamy till death at the other.

3. Regarding the mores in Europe, mistresses are accepted if they aren't flaunted, and in the States we have the Mormons, with some Mormon women undisturbed by the practice and others extremely unhappy with it. In my case, I love both women (my version of love) for their similarities and differences.

Neither of them liked my proposal, but both accept it. Except for the circumstances, I believe they would enjoy each other's friendship. As things now stand, they regard each other as rivals. My problem at the moment is to convince them to forget about competition. I see them as two parts of a whole. So, if you're still working on that book about older men, Minerva, and what they desire, the preceding is grist for your mill, but don't name names.

Moses' story is proof that there is someone out there for everyone. Do you feel that I made a mistake giving him a chance? Would you have regretted such a mistake? Or could you see it as a foray into the unknown? Isn't it another marvelous trial-and-error romance that ends up as a big giggle? I've told this story so many times because this peculiar man is a creation that Chaucer might have described if he were alive today.

XXIX

The Talmud says you are rich if you are satisfied with what you have.

Stanley, a dentist who thinks of himself as normal

After reading about so many eccentrics, you are wondering if there is anyone out there who is just normal, o.k., an ordinary man. Well, I met one last night. He is a friend of a friend and lovely man who is just right for a great many American women. He is handsome at 78, white-haired with a large smile and a raucous laugh. He eats normally, watching his weight. He loves the outdoors and is healthy. "An athletic supporter," he quips. He plays golf quite a bit and still goes skiing with his sons and their sons.

One of his ancestors was a general in the American Revolution, but an alcoholic. That's probably why he grew up in a family that was careful about excess. He said his father and mother were great parents, generous, kind, hardworking, all-American good stock. In fact, after he graduated from dental school, he wanted to buy a house in a good neighborhood. His parents gave him $2,000 for a down payment. He didn't realize at the time that they only had $6,000 in life savings. He learned later after they died that they gave him one third of their assets so that he could have the house he wanted.

I learned from my friend that he had helped out his wife's relatives financially several times. When I asked if money was ever a problem, he said it wasn't. He believed the best check you could ever write would be a rubber check for the funeral director. He intended to use his money for himself and his beloved, enjoying life to the end.

This was a man who had suffered because his wife had died slowly over a period of thirteen years. She had a progressive palsy, which was quite rare, and she lost her ability to use her muscles, including her speech muscles. He built an apartment on the side of his house for helpers who could assist him in caring for her. No, he wasn't lonely. She was there and could understand him when he spoke to her. He loved her and tried to take her on trips to Thailand, and the Philippines, until she couldn't handle it anymore.

"I didn't feel deprived. I tried to keep up my end of things by continuing to play golf and do what I had to do to take care of myself. Life was pretty normal. Nothing too different. I met my wife when I was one and a half years old. My father and her father were in a store together and they put us up on the counter and we played together. She was my high school sweetheart and we married when I was studying dentistry. She taught mathematics. But after we had children, she happily took care of them and me."

I asked him how long she had been dead and he said two years.

"So you didn't date anyone before you met your current girl friend?" I asked.

"No," he answered, "I met Evelyn just a few months ago. She belongs to my club but she doesn't play golf that much. One day someone introduced her to me. And I liked her. She was a nurse, you know, just like my mother. She's a lovely person, don't you think? And she has three wonderful kids whom I've met. I tease her a lot and she's become impervious to my darts. In fact, I told her I didn't like what she wore to your party the other night. And you know what she said? She didn't like the dress either."

I told him I was pleased to see that they were getting along so well, even though he was a Republican and she was a Democrat. I asked him if his parents ever fought. He said he couldn't use that word. They might have had heated discussions but not fights. They were great people, he reiterated, they were great people and her folks were great people. And most of the people he knew were great people, supportive of him and his dying wife. He had no complaints.

As for his common interests with Evelyn, she was more of a reader than he was. She could read three books a week. And she also liked to go to movies a lot more than he did. She even liked the ballet, and "stuff" like that. He had always read lots of newspapers and tried to read all the journals to keep up with his field. Besides, he'd been on a lot of boards and he had had many responsibilities in the community.

"Well, give me an example of some community activity you really enjoyed doing," I asked.

"I loved working on Sister Cities International, for example. I set up a sister city with a French town and I learned to speak and read French. The whole point to this organization is that American cities should have sister cities around the world to promote peace and friendship. It's a program that started with President Eisenhower and it still exists. In fact, Evelyn and I are going to France this summer to try to set up another such liaison. The object of the game is to increase respect, understanding and cooperation—one individual, one community at a time."

Finally, Stanley concluded our interview by telling me he was surprised that he had so much to talk about. After all, he was just a normal, ordinary guy.

I assured him that he was extraordinary because he was single, healthy, wealthy and wise. In fact, I learned later that he flew his own plane, that he was a shrewd investor, that he loved Mark Twain and that he had won a high school dance competition.

"Stanley, there are very few men your age who are still alive, single, and can dance."

"Well, maybe that's why Evelyn likes me. She loves to dance."

I left him, thinking, " I wish there were more men like him. Look at what has happened. He's found someone already. But he clearly wasn't looking. He never went through phases. He never dated "nymphets." He found a "lovely" woman without really trying. May they stay satisfied with each other and their new life together."

XXX

CONCLUSION

There is life after sixty. There is the possibility of joy and even bliss. There is a future, a romantic future, if only you'll work hard enough to find a truly compatible friend. Sometimes working hard enough is just going to a meeting about some local political controversy. Sometimes it means going to a seminar on film or art or conservation. Sometimes it means giving your time to a worthy cause or going on a cruise or learning to play chess. One of my male friends said to me, "I can tell you how to find single men over sixty. Join a chess group. They're all older guys who are divorced or widowers."

In fact, the October/November, 2003 issue of "Modern Maturity Magazine" gives you a list of places where you can meet single older men. You can find this list at www.aarpmagazine.org. You can also go on line and find other suggestions under single dating services. I'm including a list of how and where to meet single men in my appendix. The list grows daily and it's become a big business, down to services that help you create advertisements. I also provide you with a questionnaire, which will help you do just that.

I am sure you've heard lots of stories of how Harry met Sally in a retirement community. Well, it happens all the time. A friend might introduce you, a relative or a neighbor. That's the easiest and best way. A boy friend from high school or college days might hear that you're single again. But that's a long shot. The short shots involve going on trips with other singles or finding someone in your church group or synagogue, in your yoga class, or on a jazz cruise. Again, do read the November issue of "Modern Maturity," the article that lists a number of ways to meet your "Perfect Mate."

Of course, I do not stress perfection. I am emphasizing compromise and modifying your expectations. If you've found some of the men I've portrayed "weird" or "beyond the pale," remember that I'm not promising rose gardens and prince charmings. In fact, it was a lot of work, the process of finding my Jack. But it was worth it!.

BE BOLD! DO IT. DON'T BE AFRAID. JOIN DATING SERVICES. TRAVEL. LEARN NEW SKILLS. BE WITH PEOPLE WHO ARE LOOKING FOR THE SAME THING YOU ARE LOOKING FOR, PEOPLE WITH THE SAME INTERESTS.

ACCEPT COMPANIONSHIP, FRIENDSHIP, WARMTH, HUMAN ATTACHMENT. DON'T KEEP LOOKING FOR AN ILLUSORY ONCE-IN-A-LIFETIME-LOVE.

Above all, consider friendship. What's wrong with a deep friendship? Just a perfect blendship?

I have a young friend who is very beautiful and talented. She has requirements for a partner, which will never be met. Not only must the man be intelligent, handsome, wealthy, gentle, and honest, but also he has to speak French fluently and he can't have any children. I know a fifty-year-old man whom I'd like to introduce her to who meets all of her requirements, but he can't speak French and he has five children from a previous marriage. A less narcissistic woman would grab him and welcome the opportunity to care for his family.

IF YOU ARE SERIOUS ABOUT FINDING A PARTNER, A SIGNIFICANT OTHER, A TRAVEL COMPANION, A LOVER, A FRIEND, OR A SPOUSE, HERE ARE MY FINAL SUGGESTIONS:

1. Accept differences. Don't limit yourself to women or men of the same religious, political, cultural or economic persuasions. Don't look for the familiar, even though that is your tendency. With maturity comes tolerance for some of us.

2. Accept imperfections. Don't idealize your late spouse. I've never met a perfectionistic person who didn't infuriate his or her partner. Expect the dark side to emerge sooner or later. Don't try to mask your own weaknesses.

3. Be more open to new paradigms. Forget about the marriage model if you can. Forget about financial dependence if you can. Think in terms of emotional support, mutual admiration, sharing happiness, growing in spirituality, enjoying each day.

4. Be playful and adventuresome. See your senior years as times to experiment, to start new projects, to explore the world with less responsibility, less anxiety, less stress.

5.   If you're going through a difficult, disorienting period, stick to one or two rules. The one I followed was: "Be with people who uplift my spirits. Stay away from people who bring me down."

6.   Face your fears and transcend them if they are unrealistic. But make a distinction between realistic and fantastic fears. Many women are afraid of having sex with someone new after many years of being monogamous. The fear of getting a communicable disease is often realistic. Obviously, safe sex is a necessity for everyone. A man who says, "I can't wear a condom; I won't have an ejaculation," is a man you don't want to play with.

7.   See a gynecologist or your urologist about other types of fears. They can help you clear up anxieties about vaginal dryness or erectile dysfunction. Talk to other single women or men if they are good friends. You might pick up a hint or two.

8.   Face the fear of possible rejection. I know women who have been told they are "too big." Have a playful comeback for such a situation, even though you are hurt or outraged.

9.   Let go of your images and standards of long ago and far away. You're an adult and not an adolescent. I met a woman in Naples, Florida who had given up on men because of the following incident:

She was a very attractive widow, approximately sixty-five years old, well off, interesting and traumatized by an experience she had several weeks after moving to an expensive condo on the beach. She went out for a walk at twilight and decided to sit on a park bench to view an extraordinary sunset. A handsome man asked if he could sit down next to her on the public bench. She said yes. They began talking and he invited her to have dinner with him. But he added," Afterwards we can go to my apartment and have safe sex."

She was astonished, declined his invitation and ran home to call her son, a colonel in the Army, to tell him what had happened. He advised, "Mom, you should be flattered. Don't let that keep you from walking. But maybe you should avoid sitting down on benches."

It was the end of innocence. Welcome to the new world of seniors.

10.   So, be sure you know and trust the person who desires you and whom you desire. That's common sense. If it's love you're waiting for, not

desire, not a great friendship, that will be harder to find. It might take lots more time. Pleasure's easy. Friendship's easier. But love, true love, ahh, that's asking for fate or accident or mysterious synchronicity. That's asking for blindness and innocence and some "enchanted evening."

In summary, what I discovered from all my interviews is that each male had a totally different set of expectations when it came to defining what he wanted. And his definition of love, if he could define it, depended on a past that was idiosyncratic and personal.

1. Jack told you what he wanted and he found me, a loving, brainy, travel companion who would accept his individuality and who was solvent enough to keep up with his life style.

2. Francis wanted the magic of a romantic connection. He wanted true love.

3. Kevin wanted a grand passion that would allow him to stay married to his Catholic wife.

4. Samson wanted a woman with a cognitive approach who asked for his point of view. She should have a career and be as busy as he was.

5. Gregory needed a mother/wife to baby him, a woman as rich as he was and someone who would put up with his grown-up, possessive children.

6. John was looking for a superwoman, someone who could keep up with his energy level.

7. Drake needed a therapist first and then a normal wife.

8. Hollis wanted his angel in his house.

9. Joe had found his Scandinavian angel, who understood his need to be dominant.

10. Vincent found community and wanted only friendship.

11. Murray had wonderful women in his life and had deeply loved two women who had died. He was preparing for death while living fully. Certainly he was a rich partner for anyone who valued wisdom and maturity.

12. Walter was seeking cosmic consciousness and was serving tantric women in his watsu hot tub.

13. Lionel needed a wife to criticize and control.

14. Steve wanted a cheerful, optimistic lady who didn't mind picnics in the rain.

15. Gary wanted a safe woman with good manners who liked gated communities.

16. Thomas could use a rescue mother.

17. Lester would settle for an intelligent woman who would take him to the movies at night.

18. Leo wanted a good-time Dolly, 5 ft.4 inches with a good body.

19. Mitchell needed a brilliant replacement for his dancing partner.

20. Jimmy needed an injection of self-esteem, someone to build up his ego.

21. Milton had to find a person who would care whether he lived or died.

22. Charles wanted an Asian woman who knew her place.

23. Stephan wanted a traditional woman who cooked, he said. But he seemed to gravitate to prostitutes and other sex providers.

24. Peter, the peeping Tom, needed kinky women for sex games.

25. Willy, the tape bamboozler, hoped to find a woman dumb and rich enough to support his insatiable, outrageous appetites.

26. Wayne was seeking a class act who would enjoy mountain tops.

27.   Rex would probably find another South American woman who, this time, would be punctual.

28.   Moses claimed he wanted a woman with a scientific mind.

29.   Stanley had found what he wanted, "a lovely, normal woman, like his mother."

All of these individuals with their specific differences tell us that matches are not made in heaven. They are usually made like jigsaw puzzle pieces. This piece fits and that one doesn't. The star-crossed lover phenomenon is certainly not a common occurrence.

If you've come this far with me, readers, you may think that there are only 8 or 9 men worth considering in this book. Remember, all you need is one. Remember that I warned you I would show you how to spot the bad ones, the peculiar ones, the ones who might dangerous and irrevocably flawed. I want you to be realistic but not cynical.

Don't give up your interests or women friends or neglect the things and people you care about. But do add this project of finding a partner who will enrich your life.

DO IT NOW. BELIEVE YOU CAN. GIVE YOUR ATTENTION AND INTENTION TO THIS SEARCH. IT HAPPENED TO ME. IT CERTAINLY CAN HAPPEN TO YOU.

BLESS YOU FOR TRYING. HAVE FUN.

Appendix A.

Directions: Put an x next to the statements which you feel are the necessary qualities you want in a man. Put two xx's next to the statements which you feel are not as important to you. Put three xxx's next to the statements that are least important. Put nothing next to the statements that don't apply at all.

I WANT A MAN WHO:

1. Is pleased with his life. ☐ ☐ ☐

2. Feels at home in the world. ☐ ☐ ☐

3. Has a sense of humor. ☐ ☐ ☐

4. Is sensitive, heart-centered, tender, caring, kind, etc. ☐ ☐ ☐

5. Is romantic. ☐ ☐ ☐

6. Is sexy. ☐ ☐ ☐

7. Is passionate. ☐ ☐ ☐

8. Is conscious, knows himself. ☐ ☐ ☐

9. Has his own interests. ☐ ☐ ☐

10. Is wise. ☐ ☐ ☐

11. Can be alone and enjoy solitude. ☐ ☐ ☐

12. Enjoys being social. ☐ ☐ ☐

13. Is a listener. ☐ ☐ ☐

14. Is charming. ☐ ☐ ☐

15. Is honest. ☐ ☐ ☐

16. Is capable of joy. ☐ ☐ ☐

17. Is respectful of the opinions of others .... ☐ ☐ ☐

18. Is playful. .... ☐ ☐ ☐

19. Is handsome. .... ☐ ☐ ☐

20. Is rich. .... ☐ ☐ ☐

21. Loves to do the things I love to do: .... ☐ ☐ ☐

.... go to the movies.

.... go to the theatre.

.... go to museums.

.... go to concerts.

.... go to lectures.

.... other

22. Loves to travel. .... ☐ ☐ ☐

23. Is handy, likes to fix things. .... ☐ ☐ ☐

24. Loves to: .... ☐ ☐ ☐

.... Swim.

.... Hike.

.... Play tennis.

.... Bowl.

.... Dance.

.... Sail.

.... Climb Mountains.

.... Do yoga.

.... Give and/or receive massages

25. Speaks well. .... ☐ ☐ ☐

26. Writes well. .... ☐ ☐ ☐

27. Reads a lot. .... ☐ ☐ ☐

28. Loves children. .... ☐ ☐ ☐

29. Loves animals. .... ☐ ☐ ☐

30. Will adore me. .... ☐ ☐ ☐

31. Enjoys music. .... ☐ ☐ ☐

32. Sings. .... ☐ ☐ ☐

33. Plays an instrument. .... ☐ ☐ ☐

34. Dresses well. .... ☐ ☐ ☐

35. Has excellent hygiene. .... ☐ ☐ ☐

36. Is orderly in his personal surroundings. .... ☐ ☐ ☐

37. Is spiritual. .... ☐ ☐ ☐

38. Is flexible. .... ☐ ☐ ☐

39. Is balanced about giving and receiving. .... ☐ ☐ ☐

40. Is open to many points of view. .... ☐ ☐ ☐

41. Is generous. .... ☐ ☐ ☐

42. Is expansive. .... ☐ ☐ ☐

43. Is buoyant. .... ☐ ☐ ☐

44. Is physically healthy. .... ☐ ☐ ☐

45. Is emotionally healthy. .... ☐ ☐ ☐

46. Is fair-minded. .... ☐ ☐ ☐

47. Is adult most of the time. .... ☐ ☐ ☐

48. Has a healthy way of discharging anger. .... ☐ ☐ ☐

49. Can apologize when he's wrong. .... ☐ ☐ ☐

50. Is grateful for what he has. .... ☐ ☐ ☐

51. Sees himself as successful and accomplished. .... ☐ ☐ ☐

52. Has the same politics as I have. .... ☐ ☐ ☐

53. Trusts me with finances. .... ☐ ☐ ☐

54. Tells me how much he appreciates me. .... ☐ ☐ ☐

55. Accepts my freedom to do what I need to do for myself. ... ☐ ☐ ☐

56. Is of the same religion. .... ☐ ☐ ☐

57. Is of the same ethnic background. .... ☐ ☐ ☐

58. Is complementary to me. .... ☐ ☐ ☐

59. Is well educated. .... ☐ ☐ ☐

60. Has assets that are substantial for rainy days. .... ☐ ☐ ☐

HE SHOULD NOT BE:

1. Controlling. .... ☐ ☐ ☐

2. A born-again anything. .... ☐ ☐ ☐

3. Excessively stubborn. .... ☐ ☐ ☐

4. Cheap. .... ☐ ☐ ☐

5. An addict. .... ☐ ☐ ☐

6. Fearful of new experiences. .... ☐ ☐ ☐

7.	Right all the time.	☐ ☐ ☐
8.	An excessive TV watcher.	☐ ☐ ☐
9.	Obsessed by his work, finances, sex, sports, etc.	☐ ☐ ☐
10.	Overly egotistical.	☐ ☐ ☐
11.	Needing, needing, needing.	☐ ☐ ☐
12.	A hypochondriac.	☐ ☐ ☐
13.	Jealous without cause.	☐ ☐ ☐
14.	A man with false teeth or a hairpiece.	☐ ☐ ☐
15.	Sarcastic.	☐ ☐ ☐
16.	Cruel.	☐ ☐ ☐
17.	Compulsively orderly.	☐ ☐ ☐
18.	Dominated by his children.	☐ ☐ ☐
19.	Overly critical.	☐ ☐ ☐
20.	Manipulative.	☐ ☐ ☐

OTHER

4)   Try to <u>WRITE</u> a "personal" ad using these qualities.

(For example: You might want to say:""honest, trustworthy, healthy senior with assets for a rainy day." But you might think twice about putting""assets" into an ad. You can find out about assets later after knowing him, not turning him off because of your focus on money. You might want to emphasize:" kind, sexy, generous man who knows himself" in an ad. But even though his hygiene and orderliness are extremely important to you, you would not put those qualities into the ad.)

1)   <u>PLACE THE AD</u> in an appropriate journal: your alumnae magazine or "The New York Review of Books" personals.

2)   Or <u>JOIN A DATING SERVICE</u> with your preferences in your head.

3)   <u>DO A SEARCH ON THE</u> Internet to find dating services or buy a book that lists such services (<u>How to Meet a Mensch in New York</u>).

Here are a few services:

1. LifeworksDating.com (for thinking singles in New York, New Jersey and Connecticut.)

2. Date.com (2 million members).

3. eharmony.com (scientific matchmaking).

4. Kiss.com (450,000 profiles 50-65).

5. GreenSingles.com

6. Rightstuffdating.com

7. Matchmaker.com (9 million members)

8. Jewishcafe.com

Also, there are singles groups to join that are based on interests: single booklovers and single art lovers and single music lovers, etc.

And don't forget dating services that are not on the internet such as: Single Gourmets, Dinner Introductions, Luncheon Introductions, etc.

Unless you're inordinately rich, don't join services that charge $10,000 to $50,000 for three good dates. But do spend money on yourself for trips you are interested in.

And do read the November, 2003 issue of **AARP**: "The Singles Report: Where to Find Your Perfect Match."

GOOD LUCK. I'D LOVE TO KNOW WHAT HAPPENS

NOW

1) <u>LIST</u> all those qualities that are essential for you (the ones with one x) in the first 60 questions.

2) <u>RANK</u> them in an order of most important to least important.

3) <u>THINK</u> about them long and hard.